SPECTRUM®

Science Test Practice

Grade 6

Published by Spectrum®
an imprint of Carson-Dellosa Publishing LLC
Greensboro, NC

Editor: Karen Thompson

Spectrum®
An imprint of Carson-Dellosa Publishing LLC
P.O. Box 35665
Greensboro, NC 27425 USA

ISBN 0-7696-8066-6

03-083147784

Table of Contents
Grade 6

SCIENCE TEST PRACTICE
Table of Contents
Grade 6

ABOUT THIS BOOK

Science Test Practice is for everyone who wants to have a working knowledge of the fundamentals of science. Written with the goal of helping students achieve on science tests, it approaches science through the format of the National Science Education Standards.

The National Science Education Standards were developed by the National Academy of Science, an organization of the leading scientists in the United States. Their goal is for all students to achieve scientific literacy. To be scientifically literate means to be able to understand the richness of the world around us; to be able to make decisions based on the skills and processes that science teaches us; and to approach problems and challenges creatively.

This book is divided into four sections, each one based on a National Science Education Content Standard. This book focuses on content standards A-D: Science as Inquiry, Physical Science, Life Science, and Earth and Space Science, with one section devoted to each standard. Standards E-G, which cover science and technology and science in personal and social perspectives, are covered within the four sections. A correlation chart details the coverage of all standards in the book (see pp. 7-8).

How to Use the Book

Students can begin with the Pretest (pp. 9-14). This test covers all the three major strands of science:

- physical science, which includes how objects move and interact;
- life science, which includes animals, plants, and ecosystems;
- earth and space science, which includes rocks and minerals, the oceans, and the solar system.

After the Pretest, you may wish to complete the test prep practice in order, or complete the sections out of sequence. Before completing the practice pages, students should read *Hints and Strategies for Answering Questions* on page 6.

Finally, the Posttest (pp. 86-91) gives students a chance to practice yet again, applying the knowledge gleaned from the rest of the book. A complete answer key appears at the back of the book.

With its real-life questions and standards-based approach, *Science Test Practice* will engage students; give them solid test-taking hints and practice; and provide them an opportunity to build their confidence for other exams.

Multiple Choice

When you encounter a multiple-choice item, read the question carefully until you are sure of its meaning. After reading the question, read all answer choices carefully. Remember that only one answer is absolutely correct; this will be the one that appears to be the truest. Rule out the answer choices that are obviously wrong and choose the answer that holds true for the science scenario, based on what you have studied. Sometimes you will need to refer to a passage or diagram to find the information you need.

Fill-in-the-Blank

When you have to fill in the blanks in a sentence, paragraph, or diagram, read the entire item carefully. Then read it a second time, pausing to think about the missing words or phrases. You can then begin to plug in the words of which you are certain. If you are not sure about a word or phrase, look for clues in other words of the sentence or paragraph. If a Word Bank is provided, cross out each word as you use it. Remember that the missing words or phrases must agree with the articles and verbs in the sentence.

Short Response

A short response answer usually includes three to four sentences. When you encounter a short response item, read the question carefully. If necessary, return to a passage or diagram to find relevant information. When you are ready to respond, try to think about one topic sentence that can summarize your answer. Write it down, then add two or three sentences that support your topic sentence.

Extended Response

An extended response, or essay, includes three parts: an introduction where you state your main idea or position, a body where you add details that support your topic idea, and a conclusion where you summarize your topic idea. When you have to write an extended response, read the question carefully. Decide whether you have to write a narrative based on a passage or diagram, or argue your point of view on a subject. Then write an introductory paragraph that explains the topic you want to discuss. In the body of the essay, try to be clear and concise, including only information that is necessary and supports the topic.

National Science Education Content Standards Correlation

As a result of activities in grades 5-8, all students should develop an understanding of the concepts below.

Standard	Pages
CONTENT STANDARD A: Science as Inquiry	
Abilities necessary to do scientific inquiry	15-25, 28
To learn about the world in a scientific manner, students need to learn how to ask questions, formulate possible answers, devise experiments to test those answers, and base their conclusions on evidence.	
Understanding about scientific inquiry	26-29, 33, 34
Students need to understand that the investigations used to gather information depend on the question being asked; that scientists use mathematics and technology as they work; and that scientists build on the work other scientists have done, by asking questions about that work and that grow out of that work.	
CONTENT STANDARD B: Physical Science	
Properties and changes of properties in matter	15, 16, 26, 27, 32-37
Motion and forces	23, 38-40
Transfer of energy	41-45
CONTENT STANDARD C: Life Science	
Structure and function in living systems	21, 46-51, 67, 68
Reproduction and heredity	52-56
Regulation and behavior	57, 61, 62, 66
Populations and Ecosystems	58-62
Diversity and adaptations of organisms	47, 51, 53, 67–70
CONTENT STANDARD D: Earth and Space Science	
Structure of the earth system	71-80
Earth's history	69, 70, 73, 74
Earth in the solar system	69, 81-85

National Science Education Content Standards Correlation continued

CONTENT STANDARD E: Science and Technology	
Abilities of technological design	30, 31, 45, 76
Understandings about science and technology	30, 31, 45, 76
CONTENT STANDARD F: Science in Personal and Social Perspectives	
Science can seem removed from everyday life, but it actually surrounds us. Personal hygiene activities are based on scientific reasoning. Understanding the risks and benefits in the world makes students more informed citizens.	
Personal health	51, 63, 64, 65
Populations, resources, and environments	45, 61, 62, 66, 69, 77
Natural hazards	63, 69
Risks and benefits	63, 69
Science and technology in society	30, 31, 45, 76
CONTENT STANDARD G: History and Nature of Science	
Science as a human endeavor	30, 31, 51, 69, 70, 76, 77
Science is a pursuit of human beings, with many different skills, backgrounds, qualities, and talents. However, scientists all share curiosity about the world, a tendency to ask questions about what is known, an openness to new ideas, insight, and creativity.	
Nature of science	16, 17, 23-25, 27, 51
History of science	16, 30, 31, 70, 76

Name____________________________ Date______________

Grade 6 Pretest

Directions: Read the questions. Choose the truest possible answer.

1. **Which of the following animals would biologists classify as being the most closely related to humans?**
   - (A) a mouse
   - (B) a chimpanzee
   - (C) a lion
   - (D) a giraffe

2. **Which word describes all animals?**
   - (F) predator
   - (G) omnivore
   - (H) autotroph
   - (J) heterotroph

3. **Which of these has an exoskeleton, meaning it has no internal bones?**
   - (A) humans
   - (B) chickens
   - (C) fish
   - (D) ants

4. **A cactus without its spines has an increased likelihood of ________ .**
   - (F) growing very tall
   - (G) being a different color than other cacti
   - (H) being eaten by desert animals
   - (J) surviving without water

5. **What do plant cells have that makes them different from animal cells?**
   - (A) chloroplasts, which use the sun's energy to make food
   - (B) mitochondria, which use sugars to provide energy for cells
   - (C) nuclei, which hold genetic information and tell the cells what to do
   - (D) cytoplasm, which is the watery substance that fills the inside of cells

6. **Which is an example of an animal using camouflage?**
   - (F) a frog using its long tongue to catch a fly
   - (G) a lizard losing its tail when grabbed from behind
   - (H) a moth that is colored exactly like the tree it lives on
   - (J) a rattlesnake warning enemies to stay away with its rattle

7. **If you put the following living things into a food chain, which would be at the top?**
   - (A) a tree
   - (B) an ant
   - (C) a bird
   - (D) a cat

Name____________________________ Date______________

Grade 6 Pretest

8. If a student drops a beaker and it shatters all over her table, she should ________ .

- Ⓕ move to another table
- Ⓖ immediately tell the teacher
- Ⓗ carefully pick up the pieces with her hand
- Ⓙ continue working and clean up the glass later

9. Which of the following is it acceptable to wear when performing an experiment?

- Ⓐ sandals
- Ⓑ shorts
- Ⓒ jewelry on the hands
- Ⓓ prescription glasses

10. Before performing an experiment, a student should ________ .

- Ⓕ make a hypothesis
- Ⓖ form a conclusion
- Ⓗ share the results
- Ⓙ analyze the results

11. Which of the following is a testable hypothesis?

- Ⓐ Apples are the best tasting fruit.
- Ⓑ Red apples are more attractive than green apples.
- Ⓒ Plants grown in the dark will produce less fruit.
- Ⓓ Plants are easier to care for than pets.

12. If you are reading a scientist's notes about an experiment, which type of measurement would you most likely see?

- Ⓕ 50 pounds
- Ⓖ 50 meters
- Ⓗ 50 gallons
- Ⓙ 50 handfuls

13. A graduated cylinder is best used for measuring the ________ of a liquid.

- Ⓐ height
- Ⓑ mass
- Ⓒ volume
- Ⓓ weight

GO ON

Name______________________________ Date______________

Grade 6 Pretest

Directions: Write F if the statement is false and T if it is true.

_____ **14. The earth's axis is tilted.**

_____ **15. The earth's orbit is perfectly circular.**

_____ **16. The moon revolves around the earth.**

_____ **17. The earth is the center of the universe.**

_____ **18. The sun is the largest star in the universe.**

_____ **19. Most of the universe is empty space.**

_____ **20. The sun's gravity keeps the earth in its orbit.**

_____ **21. Jupiter is the largest planet in our solar system.**

_____ **22. The sun is the largest object in our solar system.**

_____ **23. The earth revolves around the sun once every 24 hours.**

_____ **24. Our solar system is part of the Andromeda Galaxy.**

_____ **25. The earth is the closest planet to the sun in our solar system.**

_____ **26. The earth is the only planet in our solar system with a moon.**

_____ **27. The earth is traveling through space at incredibly high speeds (thousands of miles per hour).**

_____ **28. The equator is hotter than the North and South Poles because it is closer to the sun than either pole.**

_____ **29. When it is summer in the Northern Hemisphere of the earth, it is winter in the Southern Hemisphere.**

_____ **30. Saturn is the furthest planet from the sun in our solar system.**

_____ **31. Asteroids are most commonly found on the surface of the earth's moon.**

Name____ Date__________________

Grade 6 Pretest

Directions: Match each word with its definition by writing the correct letter in the blanks provided.

_____ **32. Lava**

_____ **33. Mantle**

_____ **34. Magma**

_____ **35. Erosion**

_____ **36. Igneous**

_____ **37. Inner core**

_____ **38. Outer core**

_____ **39. Weathering**

_____ **40. Richter scale**

_____ **41. Metamorphic**

_____ **42. Sedimentary**

_____ **43. Tectonic plates**

_____ **44. Divergent boundary**

_____ **45. Convergent boundary**

_____ **46. Transform plate boundary**

Ⓐ made of liquid metals

Ⓑ most likely made of solid iron and nickel

Ⓒ tectonic plates grind past one another

Ⓓ tectonic plates collide with one another

Ⓔ melted rock that is beneath Earth's surface

Ⓕ the layer of Earth directly beneath the crust

Ⓖ melted rock that reaches Earth's surface

Ⓗ tectonic plates move away from one another

Ⓘ process of breaking rocks into smaller pieces

Ⓙ a measurement of the energy released by an earthquake

Ⓚ process of moving small rocks and sand to new locations

Ⓛ type of rock that forms when clay and sand is pressed together

Ⓜ type of rock that forms when magma or lava cools and hardens

Ⓝ large segments of Earth's outer crust upon which continents and oceans rest

Ⓞ type of rock that forms when other types of rock are put under intense pressure and heat

Name________________________________ Date______________

Grade 6 Pretest

Directions: Read the text below and study the graph. Use information from both to help you answer questions 47–48.

Not getting enough sleep at night can slow our reflexes and make it harder for us to think clearly. Below is a graph of an experiment performed on 5 groups of 20 students. Each group was assigned a specific number of hours to sleep, ranging from one hour to nine hours. After each group slept for their assigned number of hours, they were given a test.

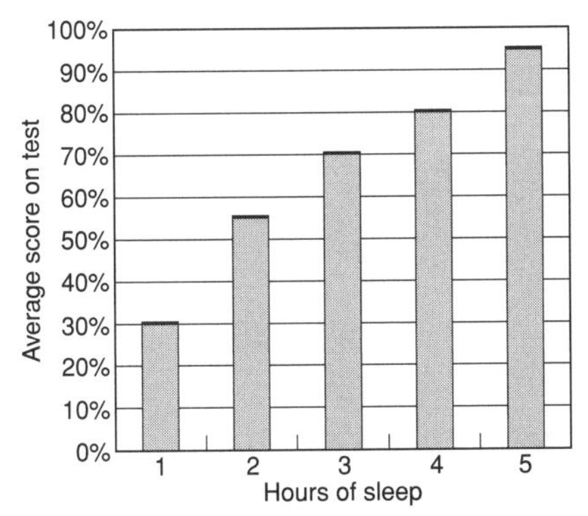

47. If a student scored 52% on the test, how many hours did the student *most likely* sleep the night before?

- Ⓕ 1
- Ⓖ 3
- Ⓗ 5
- Ⓙ 7

48. The greatest change in average score occurred between which two groups?

- Ⓐ 1 hour and 3 hours
- Ⓑ 3 hours and 5 hours
- Ⓒ 5 hours and 7 hours
- Ⓓ 7 hours and 9 hours

Directions: Study the chart below. Use information from the chart to help you answer questions 49–51.

This pie chart shows the favorite desserts of students in one school.

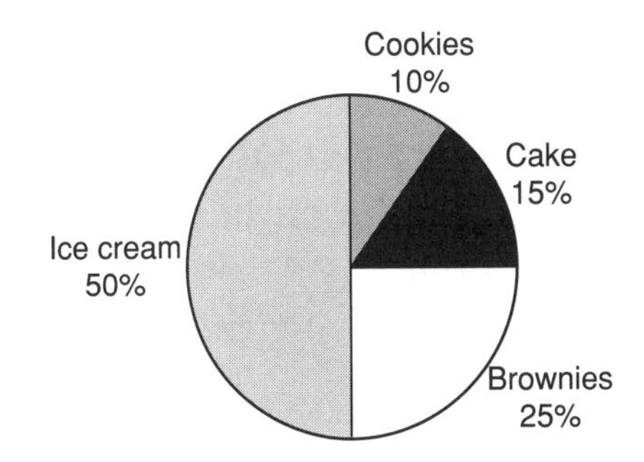

49. Which two desserts are the favorites of three-quarters of the students surveyed?

- Ⓕ cookies and cake
- Ⓖ brownies and ice cream
- Ⓗ brownies and cookies
- Ⓙ cake and brownies

50. If Grace likes the second most popular type of dessert, which dessert does she like?

- Ⓐ cookies
- Ⓑ cake
- Ⓒ brownies
- Ⓓ ice cream

51. If there are 200 students in the school, about how many of them chose cookies as their favorite dessert?

- Ⓕ 10
- Ⓖ 15
- Ⓗ 20
- Ⓙ 30

GO ON

0-7696-8066-6—*Science Test Practice*

Name______________________________________ Date________________

Grade 6 Pretest

Directions: Read each question. Write your answers on the lines provided.

52. **Driving to school one day, Natalie asks her mom, "Where does gasoline come from?" Her mom replies, "We can thank plants and animals for our gasoline." What does Natalie's mom mean?**

____

____

53. **Natalie wonders out loud, "How does gasoline work?" Her mom replies, "Gasoline in a car is like the lunch in your lunchbox." What does Natalie's mom mean?**

____

____

54. **Natalie then asks her mom, "How do plants get the energy that ends up in gasoline?" How should Natalie's mom reply?**

____

____

55. **As they continue driving to school, Natalie looks out the window and notices a dam blocking a river. She asks her mom what the dam is used for, and her mom says it makes electricity. How does that happen?**

____

____

56. **"One more question, Mom," says Natalie. "Can resources such as rivers and trees be used up the same way that gasoline can?" How should Natalie's mom reply?**

____

____

STOP

Name______________________________ Date______________

Grade 6

Directions: Read each question. Write your answer on the lines provided.

1. **Why is this lab area an unsafe place to perform an experiment?**

____

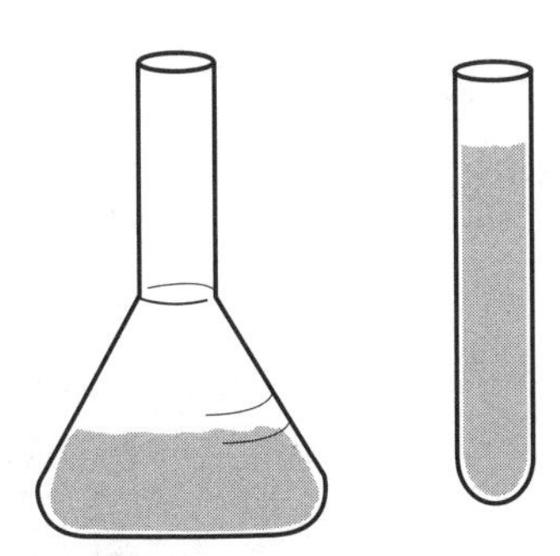

2. **What protective equipment should be put on before mixing these chemicals?**

____

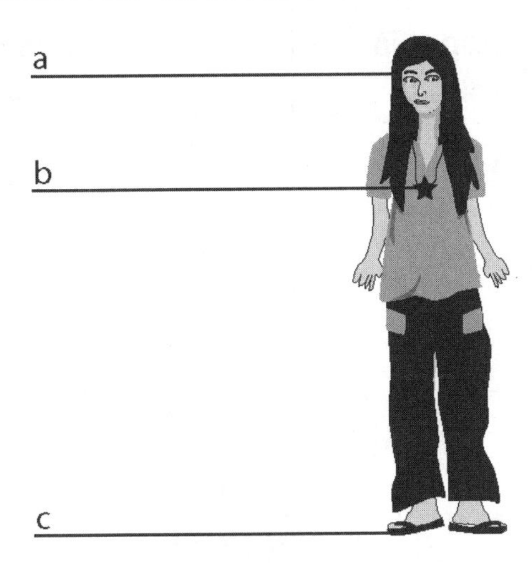

3. **Label the potential hazards if the student above is to perform a science experiment.**

STOP

Name________________________________ Date______________

Grade 6

Directions: Read the text below. Then match each statement with the number of the correct step in the scientific method.

The scientific method is a set of steps that scientists use in order to learn more about something. By following the scientific method, scientists can gather information, perform experiments, and discover new things about our world. The scientific method follows this general pattern:

1. **make observations about our world**
2. **identify a problem or question**
3. **research information about that problem or question**
4. **make an educated guess about the problem or question**
5. **design and perform an experiment**
6. **gather and study new information from the experiment**
7. **think about and draw conclusions from the new information**

_____ **Elissa hypothesizes that crickets make more noise on hot nights than on cool nights.**

_____ **Elissa counts the number of chirps made by two groups of crickets, one group in a cool cage and one group in a warm cage.**

_____ **Elissa goes to the library to read information in an encyclopedia about the habits of crickets.**

_____ **Elissa wonders what causes crickets to make more noise some nights than others.**

_____ **Elissa makes a chart of the number of chirps made by the crickets in the cool cage versus the number of chirps made by the crickets in a warm cage.**

_____ **Elissa concludes that crickets chirp more often on hot nights than on cool nights.**

_____ **Elissa notices that during the summer, crickets make a lot of noise some nights, and little noise other nights.**

STOP

0-7696-8066-6—*Science Test Practice*

Name______________________________ Date________________

Grade 6

Directions: Read the text below. Use information from the text to help you answer questions 1–2.

Cheng has difficulty sleeping during the summer because her pillow gets too hot and becomes uncomfortable. She decides to conduct an experiment to determine which type of pillow will stay the coolest.

1. **Cheng has already identified a problem, so now she needs to research the problem. How can she find out what types of pillows are being made?**

____

____

____

2. **Cheng finds out that there are four main types of pillows: wool, cotton, foam, and feather. Now she needs to form a hypothesis. Which type of pillow do you think will stay the coolest and why?**

____

____

____

Cheng then plans an experiment to test which type of pillow will stay the coolest. She places a small amount of wool, cotton, foam, and feathers underneath a heat lamp. Beneath each material, she places a thermometer. After 20 minutes, she records the temperature of each material.

Directions: Read each statement below. Place an "X" next to the sentence if it describes something Cheng SHOULD do in the experiment.

3. ____ **a. Use the same amount of material for each of the four pillow types.**

____ **b. Make the distance between the lamp and each material the same.**

____ **c. Use a different type of bulb for each material tested.**

____ **d. Stretch out the wool and cotton samples, and compress the foam and feather samples.**

Directions: Study the table below. Use it to help you answer question 4.

4. **Results:**

Pillow Type	**Temperature**
Cotton	23.8°C
Wool	26.6°C
Foam	25.9°C
Feather	25.1°C

Based on the results, which type of pillow should Cheng use to stay cooler?

____

STOP

Name________________________________ Date________________

Grade 6

Directions: Read the text below. Then fill in the table as directed.

When measuring different quantities of objects, scientists must record their data using the correct units so others can understand what their data means. Scientists have agreed to use SI units.

1. **Common SI units of measurement are listed in the Word Bank below. Write each measurement in the appropriate spot on the grid below.**

Word Bank

kilometers per hour | kilogram | meter | liter | degrees Celsius

Length	Mass	Volume	Temperature	Rate of Travel

Directions: Based on your knowledge of SI units, fill in the missing information with one of the following: mm, cm, m, km, g, kg, mL, or L. The units may be used more than once.

2. **A carton of milk can hold 1.8 ________________ of milk, which is equivalent to 1800 ________________ of milk.**
3. **A dollar bill is about 155 ________________ long.**
4. **The distance from Earth to the moon is about 384,000 ________________ .**
5. **A paper clip weighs 1 ________________ .**
6. **When a polar bear stands on two feet, it may be as tall as 2.6 ________________ .**
7. **When a human baby is born, it may weigh about 3000 ________________, but when it grows into an adult, it can weigh 70 ________________ .**
8. **A can of soda is about 12.3 ________________ tall.**

STOP

0-7696-8066-6—*Science Test Practice*

Name____ Date____________________

Grade 6

Directions: Read the questions. Choose the truest possible answer.

1. It would make the most sense to use a microscope to look at which item?

Ⓐ a small spider
Ⓑ the tip of your pencil
Ⓒ a cheek cell
Ⓓ a maple leaf

2. What should you do if you are supposed to boil water, but your beaker has a crack on the bottom?

Ⓕ Boil the water as you would normally.
Ⓖ Boil the water using a lower temperature.
Ⓗ Tell your teacher that the beaker is cracked.
Ⓙ Throw away the beaker in the nearest garbage can.

3. Which of the following tools would be used to make an incision?

Ⓐ pins
Ⓑ forceps
Ⓒ a scalpel
Ⓓ a dropper

4. Theo has placed a thermometer in a flask of water that is heating on a burner. When the water begins to bubble and steam rises from the flask, the thermometer *most likely* reads __________ .

Ⓕ 100° C
Ⓖ 100° F
Ⓗ 150° F
Ⓙ 212° C

5. Laurel is performing an experiment that involves combining 50 mL of water with 50 g of baking soda. After measuring 50 mL of water in a graduated cylinder, which of the containers below should Laurel use for mixing together the water and baking soda?

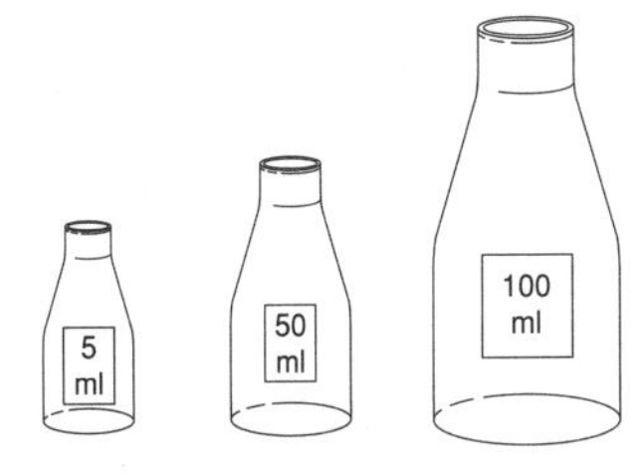

Ⓐ the 5 mL flask
Ⓑ the 50 mL flask
Ⓒ the 100 mL flask
Ⓓ the 5 mL and 50 mL flasks

6. A student places a small block of wood on the pan of a balance. He then places standard masses on the other pan. It takes 4 ten-gram masses, 1 five-gram mass, and 3 one-gram masses in order for the pans to balance out. What is the mass of the block of wood?

Ⓕ 8 g
Ⓖ 12 g
Ⓗ 48 g
Ⓙ 413 g

Name________________________ Date____________

Grade 6

Directions: Identify the parts of the microscope below by writing the correct name in the numbered spaces.

Word Bank

arm	base	coarse-adjustment knob	eyepiece
fine-adjustment knob	high-power lens	light source	low-power lens
stage			

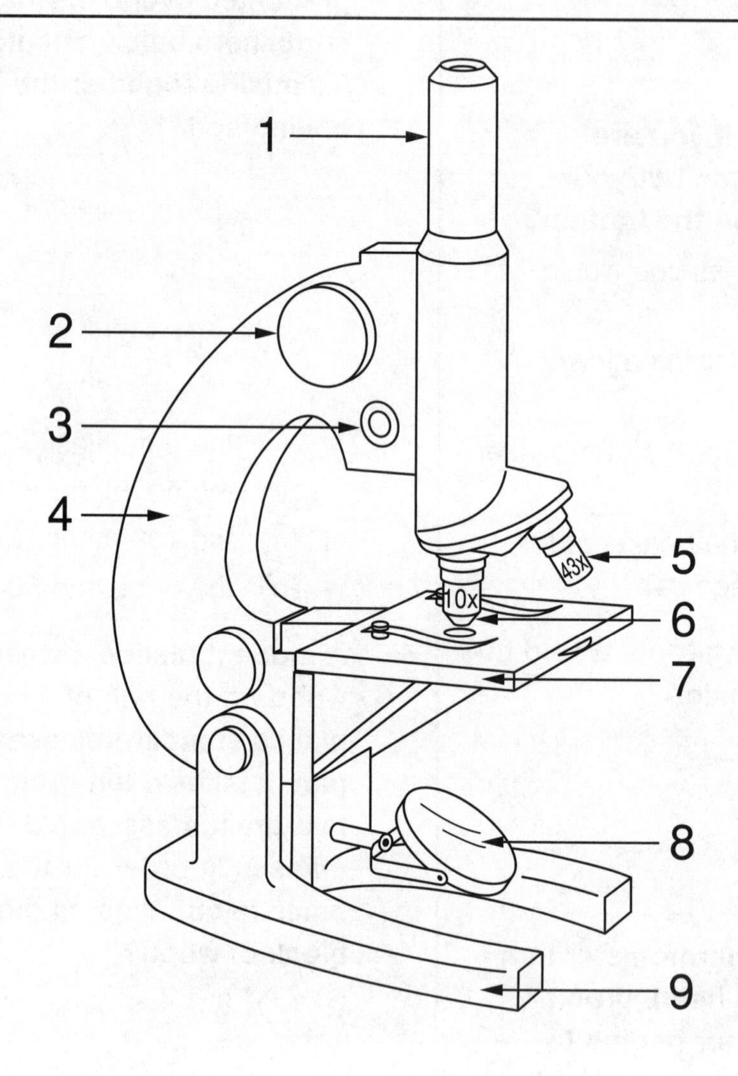

1. ____________________
2. ____________________
3. ____________________
4. ____________________
5. ____________________
6. ____________________
7. ____________________
8. ____________________
9. ____________________

STOP

Name________________________________ Date______________

Grade 6

Directions: Read the text below and study the table. Then make a bar graph that clearly shows the information in the table. Include labels and a title for your graph.

Jenny wants to buy the brand of birdseed that will attract the most birds, so she sets up an experiment to see what kind of birdseed is best. In April, she hangs four birdfeeders in her yard, each with a different type of food.

The following table shows her results for the month of April:

Type of birdseed:	Happy Bird Seed	Yummy Seed	Birds Feast Birdseed	Farmer Joes Birdseed
Number of bird visits:	25	20	5	50

STOP

Name________________________________ Date______________

Grade 6

Directions: Read the questions. Choose the truest possible answer.

1. **What is the best way to compare the size of a part to the whole?**

   Ⓐ a table
   Ⓑ a pie chart
   Ⓒ a bar graph
   Ⓓ a line graph

2. **What is the most effective way to show how a bicycle rider's speed changes over the course of his entire trip?**

   Ⓕ a table
   Ⓖ a pie chart
   Ⓗ a bar graph
   Ⓙ a line graph

3. **When performing an experiment, it is easiest to record data using __________ .**

   Ⓐ a table
   Ⓑ a pie chart
   Ⓒ a bar graph
   Ⓓ a line graph

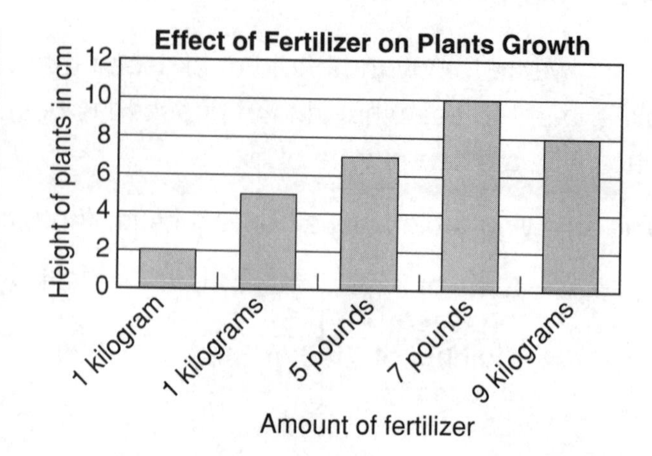

4. **What is wrong with this bar graph?**

   Ⓕ The bar for 9 kilograms of fertilizer should be taller than the bar for 7 pounds.
   Ⓖ The amount of fertilizer should be recorded in metric units only.
   Ⓗ The type of information in this bar graph should be displayed in a pie chart instead.
   Ⓙ The scale used for height should be in intervals of 20.

5. **Below is a table of distances that runners covered in a competition.**

Runner	***10 minutes***	***30 minutes***
Ben	1.5 km	5.0 km
Sudhir	1.5 km	6.5 km
Eun-ju	2.5 km	6.5 km

Which runner traveled the farthest between the 10-minute and 30-minute mark?

Ⓐ Ben
Ⓑ Sudhir
Ⓒ Eun-ju
Ⓓ not possible to tell

Name____________________ Date____________

Grade 6

Directions: Read the text below. Use information from the text to help you answer questions 1–3.

If Steve is holding a hammer and decides to let it go, the hammer will fall to the ground. Gravity exerts a downward force on the hammer, pulling it towards Earth. However, if Steve decides to place the hammer on a table instead of dropping it, the hammer will not fall to the ground. Does that mean gravity stopped causing a downward force on the hammer? No! Gravity still causes the same downward force on the hammer. The hammer is not moving downward when placed on a table because the table is exerting an upward force. The table's upward force balances the downward force caused by gravity. These balanced forces prevent the hammer from moving up or down.

1. **Steve has a bucket filled with water. He notices that if he quickly swings the bucket over his head, even though the bucket is completely upside-down when it is over his head, the water will not fall out of the bucket. Steve guesses that there must be an upward force pushing the water. Is he correct? How do you know?**

   ____

   ____

2. **Steve tosses a tennis ball into the air and notices that it slows down, stops for an instant, and then speeds up as it falls back down. During this trial, there are three main forces acting on the ball. The first is the force caused by Steve's hand on the ball. The second is the force of gravity. The third is air resistance. Explain how those three forces affect the ball as it travels upward.**

   ____

   ____

   ____

3. **Steve is trying to move a heavy desk. He pushes the desk, but it will not move. Explain why the desk will not move.**

   a. ____________________

   Steve asks his brother to help him move the heavy desk. When they push on the desk together, it moves. Explain why Steve and his brother were able to move the desk.

   b. ____________________

Name________________________ Date____________

Grade 6

Directions: Study the graph below. Use information from the graph to help you answer questions 1–6.

This graph shows the types of plants that a science class observed during a visit to the forest. The class was divided into groups and instructed to count a variety of plants.

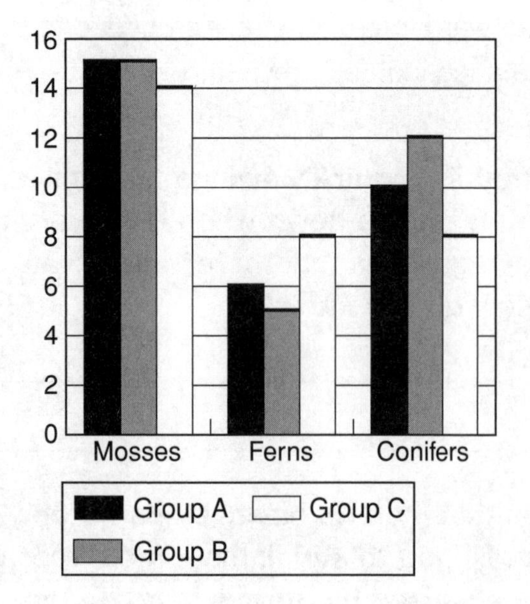

1. **Which group is represented by solid black? ________ .**

2. **Which group found the most conifers?**
________ .

3. **How many mosses did Group B find?**
   Ⓐ 15
   Ⓑ 6
   Ⓒ 12
   Ⓓ 13

4. **Which group(s) found 10 conifers?**
   Ⓕ Group A
   Ⓖ Groups B and C
   Ⓗ Group C
   Ⓙ Groups A and C

5. **Which group found the most ferns?**
________________ .

6. **What is the total number of plants found by Group B?**
   Ⓐ 15
   Ⓑ 16
   Ⓒ 19
   Ⓓ 32

STOP

0-7696-8066-6—*Science Test Practice*

Name____ Date____________________

Grade 6

Directions: Read the text below and the results. Use information from both to create a table in the space provided.

1. **Tatum studied the impact of two different types of fertilizer on the growth of plants. She had two groups of plants, each receiving one of the types of fertilizer. She recorded the average height of each group over the course of 3 weeks. In the space provided organize her results into a table so they are easier to read and understand.**

Results:

The plants receiving Brand A fertilizer were 1 cm tall at the end of week 1.
The plants receiving Brand A fertilizer were 3 cm tall at the end of week 2.
The plants receiving Brand A fertilizer were 5 cm tall at the end of week 3.
The plants receiving Brand B fertilizer were 0.5 cm tall at the end of week 1.
The plants receiving Brand B fertilizer were 1 cm tall at the end of week 2.
The plant receiving Brand B fertilizer were 2 cm tall at the end of week 3.

Name____________________ Date__________

Grade 6

Directions: Read the questions. Choose the truest possible answer.

1. **Jess measured four seeds and found their lengths to be 4.2 mm, 3.7 mm, 5.3 mm, and 4.4 mm. What was the average length of the seeds?**
   - (A) 4.3 mm
   - (B) 4.4 mm
   - (C) 4.9 mm
   - (D) 5.0 mm

2. **Manuel wanted to estimate how much water he used when he took a shower. First, he measured the time of his shower. He found that he ran the water for 7 minutes and 10 seconds. Then he held a bucket under the shower to see how much water he collected in 30 seconds. Using a measuring cup, he counted 4.25 L of water in the bucket. About how many liters of water did Manuel use during his shower?**
   - (F) 10 L
   - (G) 30 L
   - (H) 60 L
   - (J) 200 L

The graph shows the number of animals a class observed when studying a plot of land near their school.

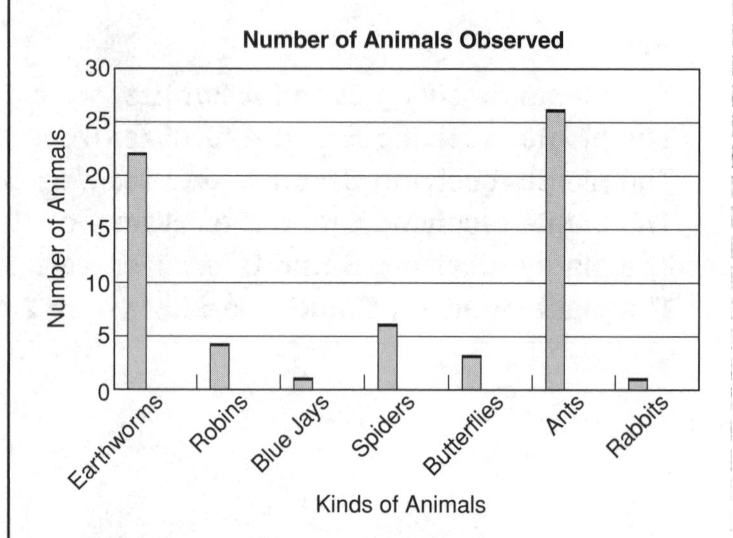

3. **What is the *best* estimation of the total number of animals the class observed?**
   - (A) 45 animals
   - (B) 55 animals
   - (C) 60 animals
   - (D) 65 animals

4. **What is the *best* estimation of the number of invertebrates, or animals without backbones, the class observed?**
   - (F) 25 invertebrates
   - (G) 45 invertebrates
   - (H) 50 invertebrates
   - (J) 55 invertebrates

Name____________________ Date____________

Directions: Read the questions. Choose the truest possible answer.

1. **On average, the bacteria E. coli can reproduce once every 20 minutes. How many times can an E. coli bacterium reproduce in 24 hours?**
   - (A) 20
   - (B) 24
   - (C) 44
   - (D) 72

2. **A Labrador retriever has a litter of 10 puppies: 2 males and 8 females. What percentage of the litter is female?**
   - (F) 20%
   - (G) 60%
   - (H) 75%
   - (J) 80%

3. **Sheng takes a 3-hour trip. During the first hour, he drives 48 miles. During the second hour, he drives 41 miles. During the last hour, he drives 61 miles. What is Sheng's average speed for this entire trip?**
   - (A) 41 mph
   - (B) 48 mph
   - (C) 50 mph
   - (D) 61 mph

4. **Julia fills a graduated cylinder with 30 mL of water. After she drops a blue marble into the cylinder, the water level rises to 42 mL. What is the volume of the marble?**
   - (F) 10 mL
   - (G) 12 mL
   - (H) 42 mL
   - (J) 72 mL

5. **Using a balance, Julia finds that the blue marble has a mass of 31.2 grams. What is the density of the blue marble? (Note: 1 mL = 1cm^3)**
   - (A) 0.4 g/cm^3
   - (B) 1.0 g/cm^3
   - (C) 2.6 g/cm^3
   - (D) 3.5 g/cm^3

6. **Julia also has a red marble with three times as much volume as the original blue marble, but exactly the same mass. This means that the red marble will be _________ .**
   - (F) 1/6 the density of the blue marble
   - (G) 1/3 the density of the blue marble
   - (H) 3 times the density of the blue marble
   - (J) 6 times the density of the blue marble

STOP

Name______________________________ Date______________

Grade 6

Directions: Read the text below. Use information from the text to help you answer questions 1–4.

Maria's Experiment

My question: I want to find out my pulse rate before exercising. Then I want to see how it changes after one minute of strenuous exercise.

What I already know: I know that my pulse tells me the rate at which my heart pushes blood through my body. My blood carries oxygen and food to my cells. It carries carbon dioxide and waste away from my cells.

What I think will happen and why: The faster my heart beats, the more oxygen and carbon dioxide my blood can carry. And when I exercise, my cells need more oxygen and food. They make more waste and give off more carbon dioxide. I hypothesize that my pulse will increase by 50% after one minute of strenuous exercise.

What I did: First, I located my pulse on my neck, near the front. Then I made a drinking straw pulse measurer so I could see my pulse. I held a piece of clay over the place on my neck where I could feel my pulse. I pushed a straw into the clay so that it stuck straight out. Then I looked in a mirror and counted the number of times the straw moved in 15 seconds. I recorded this number in a chart and multiplied it by four to find my pulse rate—the number of times my heart beats each minute.

What I found out: My pulse rate without exercising was 95 beats per minute. After running in place for one minute, it was 120 beats per minute.

1. **What can Maria conclude?**

____

2. **What can Maria do to be sure that her results are accurate and her conclusion is correct?**

____

3. **Discuss one potential problem with this experiment.**

____

4. **Maria decides that she wants to compare the pulse rate of people of different ages doing the same exercise over the same length of time. Describe in detail how she could best present the results of this extended experiment.**

____

____

Name____ Date______________

Grade 6

Directions: Read the text below. Use information from the text to help you answer questions 1–3.

Water Filtration Investigation

Tiffany and Jody wanted to enter the science fair at school. "Let's do an experiment with soil," said Jody. "We could test different kinds of soil to see how fast water moves through each one."

Tiffany and Jody went to find soil samples in order to perform their experiment. They collected samples of sand, clay, soil from a garden, and silt from a streambed. Then they spread the four kinds of soil out on paper plates.

"Look how different they are," said Jody. "Maybe we should start by recording some observations about what each type of soil looks like." Tiffany made a chart, and together they filled it in.

"Look how big the grains of sand are," said Jody. "I bet the water will travel fastest through the sand. There are so many empty spaces!"

Now the girls were ready to begin their experiment. First, they cut the bottoms out of four foam cups. Then they covered the bottom of each one with a coffee filter. Next, they taped the filters to the cups.

Jody started to put a handful of soil into one of the cups.

"Wait!" said Tiffany. "We have to measure the soil. Each cup has to have the same amount."

"You're right!" Jody put the soil back. "Let's use 100 g of each kind of soil."

"That should work," said Tiffany. They filled each foam cup with a different kind of soil. Then they put each foam cup into a clear plastic cup.

"Look," said Tiffany. "The foam cups just fit. When we pour water in, it will come out the bottom through the coffee filters and into the plastic cups."

"We'd better get a stopwatch," said Tiffany. "We can see how long it takes for the water to start coming through. We'll also need to measure how much water comes through," said Jody. "After we put the water in, let's time each cup for 5 minutes. Then we can make observations."

1. **What is the girls' hypothesis?**

   ____

2. **What is the independent variable in this experiment?**

   ____

3. **Why did Tiffany tell Jody that they had to measure the amount of soil in the cups?**

   ____

0-7696-8066-6—*Science Test Practice*

Name______________________________ Date______________

Grade 6

Directions: Read the text below. Use information from the text to help you answer the essay question. Use a separate sheet of paper if needed.

The Hubble Space Telescope

The Hubble Telescope is one of the world's most advanced and powerful telescopes. The telescope was named after Edwin Hubble, a scientist who offered evidence that the universe was expanding. Although the telescope was created after Hubble's death, it has provided much information about the unknown reaches of the universe.

The Hubble Telescope is actually orbiting 375 miles (600 km) above Earth. Even though the telescope is far from Earth, space-walking astronauts can repair and service the telescope when problems arise. Astronauts can replace equipment that is worn out. They can also upgrade instruments so they are newer and better. New technology helps create new instruments that allow the telescope to see even further into space. Scientists who designed the telescope made sure it would not become outdated. Instead, it is able to make use of the latest technology.

1. **In 2004, NASA announced that they were canceling the final servicing mission to Hubble. NASA felt that the risk to the astronauts was too great. Without this mission, Hubble would shut down in four years. Many scientists believe that steps should be taken to save the telescope. In an essay, discuss what action you think should be taken with Hubble. Explain why the telescope should or should not be saved.**

STOP

0-7696-8066-6—*Science Test Practice*

Name______________________________ Date______________

Grade 6

Directions: Read the text below. Use information from the text to help you answer the essay question. Use a separate sheet of paper if needed.

Alternate Energy Sources—Fuel

The gasoline needed to run automobiles comes from oil. Oil is a fossil fuel that will run out someday. Car manufacturers are looking for new alternative energy sources for automobiles. Experts have researched a number of potential "fuels" for the cars of the future. Some scientists predict that hydrogen may be the energy source to replace gasoline in cars. However, scientists are still working to find an energy-efficient way to produce hydrogen. In the meantime, scientists are also considering other possible energy sources, such as steam, electricity, and air. When researching an alternative fuel for cars, scientists hope to find a source that is both renewable and friendly to the environment.

1. **You are working with a team of scientists to create a car that uses an alternative energy source. Describe an idea you have for an alternative energy source to run automobiles and explain how it would work. Be sure to explain why your energy source is the best one to use.**

____

____

____

____

____

____

____

____

____

____

____

____

____

____

STOP

0-7696-8066-6—*Science Test Practice*

Name ____________________ Date ____________

Grade 6

Directions: Read the text and study the diagram below. Use information from both to help you answer questions 1–3.

Jason wanted to compare the densities of four liquids. He put 10 mL of each liquid into a graduated cylinder. Jason waited for ten minutes to allow the liquids to settle. Then he studied the cylinder shown in the picture below.

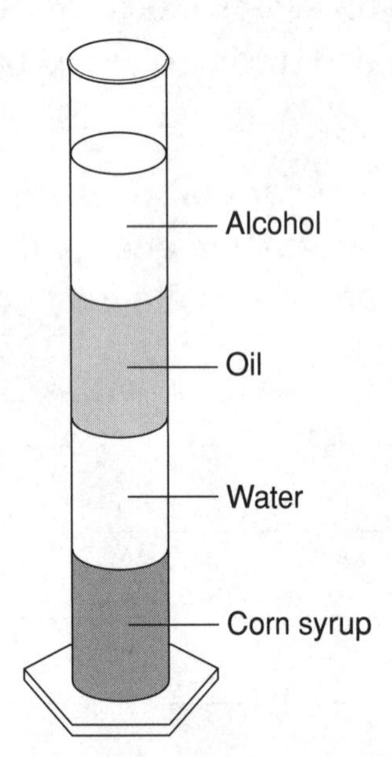

1. **Which of the liquids is the most dense?**

   ____

2. **Which liquid is more dense, water or oil?**

   ____

3. **Jason knows that the volume of each substance is 10 mL. What other quantity must he know to calculate density?**

   ____

Directions: Read the text. Use information from the text to help you answer questions 4–7.

Latisha measured the volume and mass of four cubes, each made of a different substance. Each cube had a length of 1 cm per side and a volume of 1 cm^3. The aluminum cube had a mass of 2.7 g. The copper cube had a mass of 9.0 g. The lead cube had a mass of 11.4 g. The wooden cube had a mass of 0.7 g. Latisha used the formula density=mass/volume.

4. **What is the density of copper?**

   ____

5. **What would the density of a cube of aluminum be that is 2 cm on each side?**

   ____

6. **Water has a density of 1 g/cm^3. Which of the cubes would float on the water?**

   ____

7. **Latisha was given a cube made of an unknown substance. She calculated its density to be 11.4 g/cm^3. Based on her previous calculations, what is the identity of this unknown substance?**

   ____

Name____ Date__________________

Grade 6

Directions: Study the chart below. Use the information from the chart to answer questions 1–6.

Melting Point an Boiling Points of Various Substances

Substance	Melting Point °C	Boiling Point °C
Ammonia	–78	–33
Bromine	–7	58
Lead	328	1750
Nitric acid	–42	83
Octane	–57	126
Oxygen	–218	–183
Sodium chloride	808	1465
Water	0	100

1. **Which substances are solids at room temperature (25°C)?**

   ____

2. **Your teacher has given you room temperature samples of each substance in the table above. She then asks you to pour 1 mL of the liquid substances into separate test tubes. Which substances do you pour into the test tubes?**

   ____

3. **Your teacher asks you to write a list of the substances that are gases at room temperature. Which substances do you put in your list?**

   ____

   ____

4. **As nitric acid is heated and reaches its boiling point, what happens to the nitric acid molecules?**

   ____

5. **What is the freezing point of octane?**

   ____

6. **What will happen if heat energy is added to bromine if it is applied when the substance is at room temperature?**

   ____

Name____ Date__________________

Grade 6

Directions Read the passage below. Use information from the passage to help you answer questions 1–4.

Experimenting With Mixtures

Mr. Sebastian gave his students gravel, salt, sand, and iron filings. He also gave them a hot plate, a beaker, magnets, paper plates, cups, spoons, water, a sieve, and coffee filters. He told the students to make a mixture from the four substances and then separate it.

In order to know how to separate the mixture, the students needed to know something about each of the substances. First, they tested the substances with a magnet. They placed a spoonful of each substance on a paper plate. They held a magnet near each one. The magnet did not pick up the sand, salt, or gravel, but it did pick up the iron filings.

Next, the students tested the substances in water. They mixed a spoonful of salt with warm water and stirred. They observed that the salt dissolved. Then the class mixed a spoonful of sand with water and stirred. The sand did not dissolve. They did the same thing with the gravel and the iron filings. These also did not dissolve.

Now the students were ready to make their mixture and plan how to separate it.

1. **Describe how to separate a mixture of sand and water.**

____

____

2 **One group of students creates a mixture of sand and iron filings. What steps could the group take to separate this mixture?**

____

____

3. **Your teacher gives you a mixture of water and gravel. What type of mixture is water and gravel—a suspension or a solution? Explain.**

____

____

4. **How could the students separate a mixture of salt and water?**

____

____

STOP

0-7696-8066-6—*Science Test Practice*

Name________________________________ Date________________

Grade 6

Directions: Read the questions. Choose the truest possible answer.

1. **When a substance burns, ________ .**
   - Ⓐ a physical reaction takes place
   - Ⓑ the atoms of the original substance are rearranged
   - Ⓒ a new substance is produced that has different atoms
   - Ⓓ a solution forms

2. **When elements combine to make a compound, what is true about the compound?**
   - Ⓕ The compound has the same properties as the elements it is made of.
   - Ⓖ The compound has different properties than the elements it is made of.
   - Ⓗ The elements that make the compound can be easily separated.
   - Ⓙ The elements within the compound do not exist in a set ratio.

3. **Which of the following is a chemical change?**
   - Ⓐ Copper turns green in the presence of oxygen.
   - Ⓑ An egg is cracked open.
   - Ⓒ Sugar is stirred into water and seems to disappear.
   - Ⓓ Water boils and evaporates.

4. **In a combustion reaction, a substance combines with oxygen and gives off heat. Which of the following is a combustion reaction?**
   - Ⓕ a nail rusting
   - Ⓖ an acid and a base being mixed together
   - Ⓗ a piece of paper burning
   - Ⓙ a heated gas changing into two other gases

5. **Which of the following is a compound?**
   - Ⓐ a helium atom
   - Ⓑ a cup of sand
   - Ⓒ a block of aluminum
   - Ⓓ a lump of sugar

6. **The composition of a compound ________ .**
   - Ⓕ is the same everywhere in the compound
   - Ⓖ always changes when it is heated
   - Ⓗ always changes when it is mixed with another compound
   - Ⓙ depends on the size of the sample

7. **Which of the following shows the formula for a compound?**
   - Ⓐ Zn
   - Ⓑ N
   - Ⓒ CO_2
   - Ⓓ $2H_2 + O_2 = 2H_2O$

Name ______________________________ Date ______________

Grade 6

Directions: The Word Bank contains common properties of groups of elements. Write each property in the correct place in the table below.

Word Bank

Good conductors	Lose electrons easily	Luster
Moderate conductors	Poor conductors	Tend to gain electrons

Metals	Metalloids	Nonmetals

Directions: Read the questions. Choose the truest possible answer.

2. **All of the following are properties that let you know an element is a metal except ________ .**
   - Ⓐ being able to conduct electricity
   - Ⓑ being able to bend without cracking
   - Ⓒ being shiny in appearance
   - Ⓓ being red or blue in color

3. **Which of the following is the *best* description of water?**
   - Ⓕ Water is a molecule, but not an atom.
   - Ⓖ Water is an atom, but not a molecule.
   - Ⓗ Water is both a molecule and an atom.
   - Ⓙ Water is neither a molecule nor an atom.

0-7696-8066-6—*Science Test Practice*

Name ______________________________ Date ______________

Grade 6

Directions: Read the text below and study the diagram. Use the information from both to help you answer questions 1–2.

The color of the flowers on a hydrangea bush depends on the pH of the soil. The chart below shows the flower colors at various pHs.

pH	Flower Color
4.5	deep, vivid blue
5.0	medium blue
5.5	lavender-purple
6.0	purplish-pink
6.5	mauve-pink
6.8	medium-pink
7.0	deep, vivid-pink

1. **What color would the flowers be if the bush could be grown in neutral soil, or water?**
   - (A) deep, vivid blue
   - (B) medium blue
   - (C) purplish-pink
   - (D) deep, vivid pink

2. **How does the soil that medium pink hydrangeas grow in compare to the soil that medium blue hydrangeas grow in?**
   - (F) The soil is more acidic.
   - (G) The soil is less acidic.
   - (H) The soil has the same acidity.
   - (J) The soil has no acidity.

Directions: Read the questions. Choose the truest possible answer.

3. **Which of the following statements best describes an element?**
   - (A) An element can be broken down and combined.
   - (B) An element can be broken down but cannot be combined.
   - (C) An element cannot be broken down but can be combined.
   - (D) An element cannot be broken down and cannot be combined.

4. **Organic compounds all contain the elements ________ .**
   - (F) carbon, helium, and oxygen
   - (G) nitrogen, hydrogen, and oxygen
   - (H) nitrogen, helium, and carbon
   - (J) carbon, hydrogen, and oxygen

5. **The chemical symbol "O" represents ________ .**
   - (A) the element oxygen
   - (B) a molecule of oxygen
   - (C) the compound oxygen
   - (D) the atomic number of oxygen

6. **In the periodic table, elements are grouped ________ .**
   - (F) in alphabetical order
   - (G) together if they have similar properties
   - (H) in the order in which they were discovered
   - (J) near other elements with which they easily react

Name____ Date____________________

Grade 6

Directions: Study the chart below. Use information from the chart to answer questions 1–3.

Object A		Object A	
Time (seconds)	Position (meters)	Time (seconds)	Position (meters)
0	0	0	0
1	6	1	4
2	12	2	12
3	18	3	20
4	24	4	24

1. **What is the difference in the speed of objects A and B?**

____

____

____

2. **What happens to the velocity of a car traveling at 45 miles per hour as it goes around a curve? Why does this happen?**

____

____

____

3. **Study the motion of object A over the 4-second period. How many meters would you expect object A to travel after a period of 6 seconds? Explain how you arrived at your answer.**

____

____

____

Directions: Read each question. Write your answers on the lines provided.

4. **The distance from Jessica's house to her friend Jaclyn's house is 4 km. It took Jessica 20 minutes to ride her bicycle to Jaclyn's house. What was Jessica's average speed in kilometers per hour?**

____

____

____

____

5. **Mason has a piano lesson today and he can't be late. Mason lives 5 km from his piano teacher's house. He has 15 minutes until his lesson starts. At what average speed in kilometers per hour must Mason ride his bike to arrive for his lesson in time?**

____

____

____

____

6. **Salih ran the 50-meter dash in 6.5 seconds. What was his average speed in meters per second?**

____

____

____

____

Name_______________ Date_______________

Grade 6

Directions: Study the chart below. Use information from the chart to answer questions 1–4.

Li s Family		Darrell s Family	
Time (hours)	Position (kilometers)	Time (hours)	Position (kilometers)
0	0	0	0
1	70	1	60
2	150	2	140
3	240	3	220
4	320	4	320

Li's family and Darrell's family traveled to the ocean together, but they went in separate cars. The total distance was 320 km.

1. **How does the average speed of the two families for the entire trip compare? Explain.**

____

____

2. **What was the fastest speed traveled by either family?**

____

____

3. **What was the average speed of Li's family during the first two hours?**

____

____

____

____

4. **On the trip home, Li's family traveled at an average speed of 100 km/hr. How does the family's trip home compare to their trip to the beach? Which trip most likely took the shortest amount of time?**

____

____

____

____

STOP

Name________________________________ Date______________

Grade 6

Directions: Study each diagram below. Use information from the diagrams to answer questions 1–3.

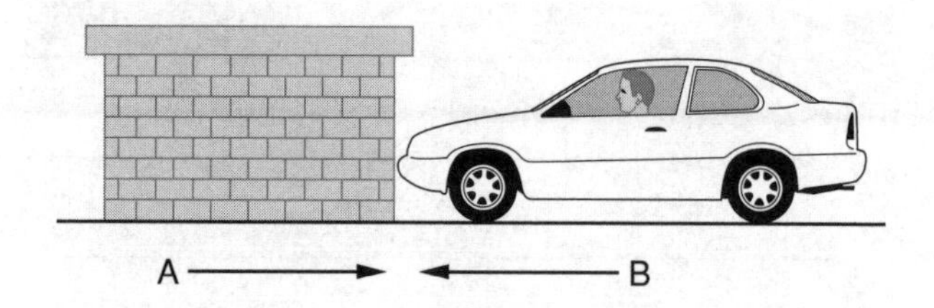

1. **What do arrows A and B represent?**

____

____

____

____

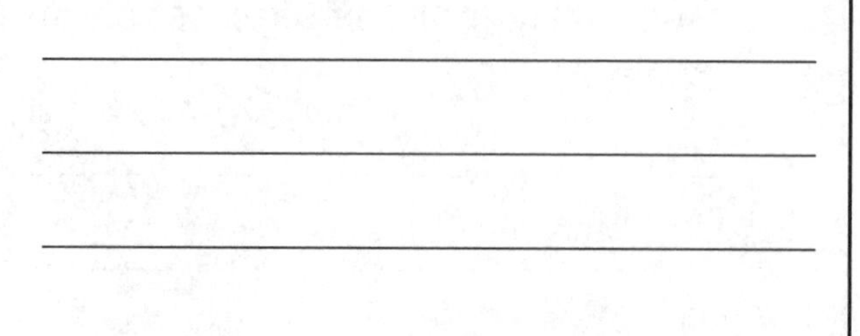

2. **What force does Arrow A represent?**

____

____

3. **Which arrow below represents the force of gravity acting on the person?**

____

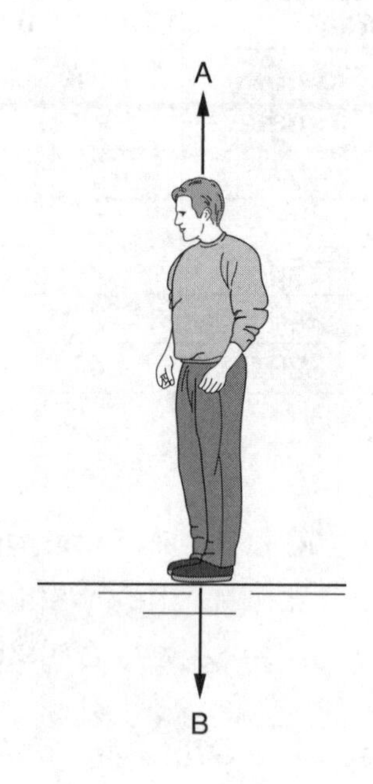

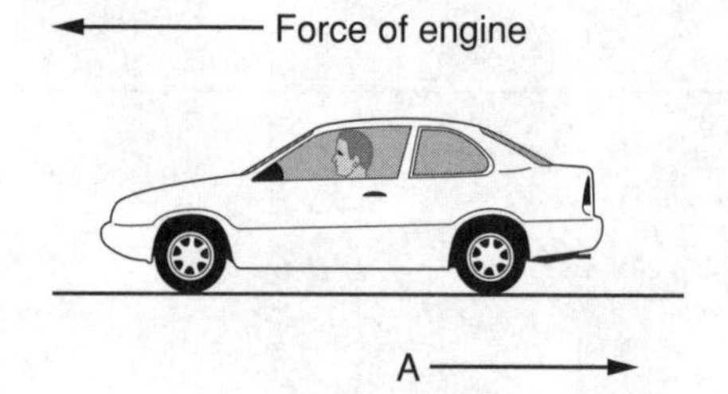

STOP

Name____ Date________________

Grade 6

Directions: Choose the correct word from the pair to complete each sentence below.

1. **Sound and light energy are carried by ________________ .**

   waves, pitch

2. **A ________________ has particles that vibrate at right angles to the direction of the wave.**

   transverse wave, longitudinal wave

3. **The number of vibrations a wave goes through in a given time is its ________________ .**

   wavelength, frequency

4. **________________ waves need to travel through matter.**

   Electromagnetic, Mechanical

5. **Radiant energy is carried by ________________ .**

   electromagnetic waves, transverse waves

6. **Solar energy reaches Earth through ________________ .**

   conduction, radiation

Directions: Read each sentence below and fill in the blanks with words from the Word Bank.

Word Bank

wavelength	compression	rarefaction
trough	crest	amplitude

7. **The highest part of a mechanical wave is called the ________________ .**

8. **The lowest part of a mechanical wave is called the ________________ .**

9. **An area of a longitudinal wave where particles are closer together is called a ________________ .**

10. **An area of a longitudinal wave where particles are more spread out is called a ________________ .**

11. **The ________________ of a wave is the distance that any single point in the wave moves from its resting position.**

12. **The distance between any two identical parts of a longitudinal wave is its ________________ .**

Name ______________________ Date ______________

Grade 6

Directions: Read the questions. Choose the truest possible answer.

1. **Which of these is a measure of thermal energy?**
   - Ⓐ volume
   - Ⓑ density
   - Ⓒ pressure
   - Ⓓ temperature

2. **By which of these processes does heat move through liquids and gases?**
   - Ⓕ convection
   - Ⓖ radiation
   - Ⓗ conduction
   - Ⓙ transition

3. **Which of the following materials is the best conductor?**
   - Ⓐ wood
   - Ⓑ plastic
   - Ⓒ metal
   - Ⓓ cloth

4. **Thermal energy moves between two objects that are touching through the process of ________ .**
   - Ⓕ radiation
   - Ⓖ convection
   - Ⓗ conduction
   - Ⓙ association

5. **An object that does not conduct heat very well is a(n) ________ .**
   - Ⓐ conductor
   - Ⓑ insulator
   - Ⓒ radiator
   - Ⓓ elastomer

6. **What causes you to get warm if you stand near a fire?**
   - Ⓕ radiation
   - Ⓖ convection
   - Ⓗ conduction
   - Ⓙ transmission

7. **When you pick up a glass of ice water, heat moves from ________ .**
   - Ⓐ the water to the ice
   - Ⓑ the ice to the water
   - Ⓒ the glass to your hand
   - Ⓓ your hand to the glass

8. **How does thermal energy travel in radiation?**
   - Ⓕ as particles
   - Ⓖ as waves
   - Ⓗ as electricity
   - Ⓙ as beams

STOP

0-7696-8066-6—*Science Test Practice*

Name ________________________________ Date ____________

Grade 6

Directions: Read the questions. Choose the truest possible answer.

1. **Light waves are ________ .**
   - Ⓐ opaque waves
   - Ⓑ longitudinal waves
   - Ⓒ transparent waves
   - Ⓓ electromagnetic waves

2. **Light waves that bounce off a surface ________ .**
   - Ⓕ reflect
   - Ⓖ refract
   - Ⓗ reradiate
   - Ⓙ reabsorb

3. **Through which of the following objects can light travel?**
   - Ⓐ a wood frame
   - Ⓑ a ceramic plate
   - Ⓒ a glass of water
   - Ⓓ a carton of milk

4. **Why does a black jacket appear black?**
   - Ⓕ It emits all the colors of light.
   - Ⓖ It reflects all the colors of light.
   - Ⓗ It refracts all the colors of light.
   - Ⓙ It absorbs all the colors of light.

5. **Imagine a spoon is sitting in a glass of water. What causes the spoon to appear bent when you look at it through the glass?**
   - Ⓐ reflection
   - Ⓑ refraction
   - Ⓒ convection
   - Ⓓ absorption

6. **What type of material scatters light so objects cannot be seen clearly through it?**
   - Ⓕ clear
   - Ⓖ opaque
   - Ⓗ translucent
   - Ⓙ transparent

7. **Which color of visible light has the longest wavelength?**
   - Ⓐ red
   - Ⓑ orange
   - Ⓒ green
   - Ⓓ blue

STOP

Name____ Date________________

Grade 6

Directions: Read the questions. Choose the truest possible answer.

1. **Electricity will only flow through a circuit if the circuit is ________.**
   - Ⓐ open
   - Ⓑ connected in series
   - Ⓒ connected in parallel
   - Ⓓ closed

2. **Electricity must travel through ________ .**
   - Ⓕ a coil
   - Ⓖ a switch
   - Ⓗ a conductor
   - Ⓙ an insulator

3. **A ________ may be used to break an electrical circuit.**
   - Ⓐ switch
   - Ⓑ battery
   - Ⓒ generator
   - Ⓓ copper wire

4. **Which of the following is caused by static electricity?**
   - Ⓕ a hydroelectric dam producing electricity
   - Ⓖ a flashlight working after a battery is inserted
   - Ⓗ a bulb giving off light when a switch is flipped
   - Ⓙ a balloon sticking to a wall after being rubbed with a cloth

5. **Which of these is a good conductor of electricity?**
   - Ⓐ wood
   - Ⓑ glass
   - Ⓒ copper
   - Ⓓ plastic

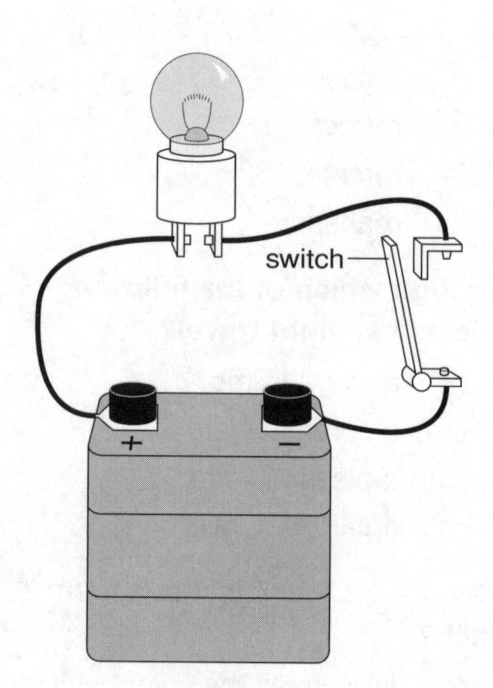

6. **In the diagram above, what must happen to make the light bulb shine?**
   - Ⓕ The switch must be closed.
   - Ⓖ The wire must be straightened.
   - Ⓗ The battery must be disconnected.
   - Ⓙ The light bulb must be screwed more tightly.

STOP

Name ______________________ Date ______________

Grade 6

Directions: Read the passage below. Use information from the passage to help you answer questions 1–2.

Solar Energy

Solar energy comes from the sun. It is solar radiation that reaches Earth. Solar energy can be changed into other forms of energy such as electricity and heat. The energy from sunlight can be captured without creating pollution. Sunlight is a renewable energy source. It will not run out for millions of years.

If solar energy is clean and renewable, why don't more people use it? First, it can be expensive to purchase the equipment needed to use solar energy. Large panels with photovoltaic cells are used to collect the sun's energy. The panels may cover a large part of the roof of a house. Their large size is necessary to collect enough solar energy to be useful.

Another disadvantage is the weather. Although the sun is a renewable resource, it does not always shine. Clouds may block the sun and, therefore, block the energy source. New technologies are being developed to make it more efficient to collect solar energy as well as store it for cloudy days.

1. **Vijay is building a tennis racket factory, but must decide if he will install solar panels to help supply his building with energy. Discuss the benefits and drawbacks of installing solar panels in his factory.**

____

____

____

____

2. **Solar energy is used to power satellites and telescopes in space. What is the main advantage of using solar energy for this instead of another energy source?**

____

____

____

____

STOP

0-7696-8066-6—*Science Test Practice*

Name______________________________ Date______________

Grade 6

Directions: Study the diagrams below and fill in the blanks with words from the Word Bank. Some of the words will be used in both diagrams.

Word Bank

cell membrane	cytoplasm	cell wall	mitochondrion	nucleolus
nucleus	vacuole	nuclear membrane	chloroplast	ribosome

Cross Section of an Animal Cell

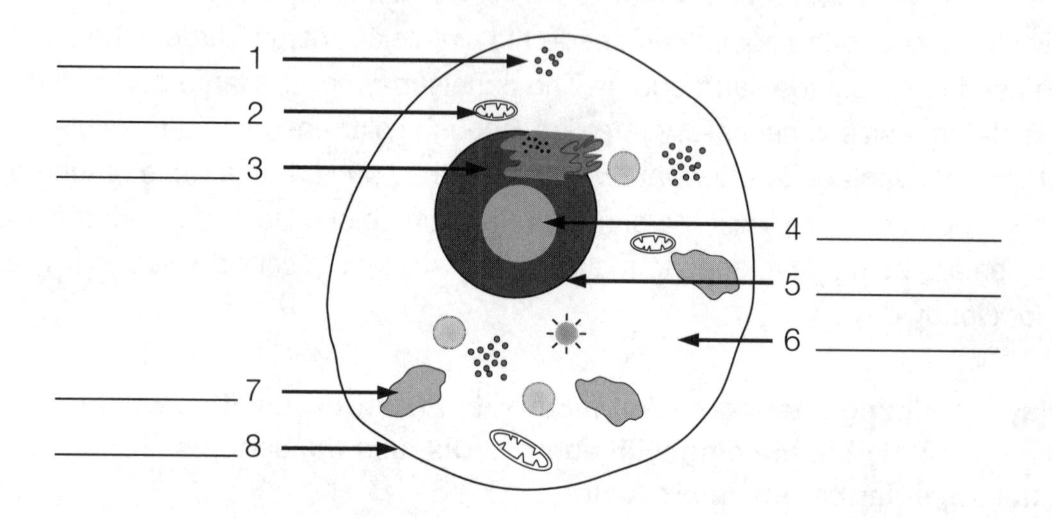

Cross Section of a Plant Cell

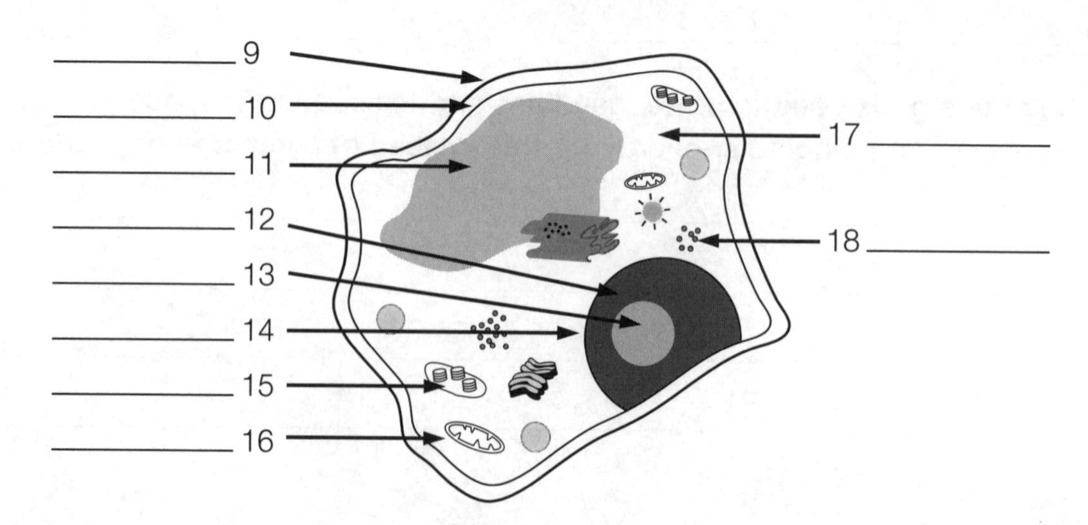

0-7696-8066-6—*Science Test Practice*

Name ____________________ Date ____________

Grade 6

Directions: Read the questions. Choose the truest possible answer.

1. **One-celled organisms may live in __________ .**
   - (A) classes
   - (B) schools
   - (C) families
   - (D) colonies

2. **How do most unicellular organisms reproduce?**
   - (F) The organisms split apart into two new cells.
   - (G) The organisms go through meiosis to form new cells.
   - (H) A male organism and a female organism unite and then split.
   - (J) The organisms split into two cells and then unite with other split cells.

3. **The cells of multicellular organisms perform different jobs. In other words, they __________ .**
   - (A) equalize
   - (B) strategize
   - (C) specialize
   - (D) categorize

4. **Which of the following is found in the cells of both unicellular and multicellular organisms?**
   - (F) cytoplasm
   - (G) a nucleus
   - (H) Golgi bodies
   - (J) a cell wall

5. **Which of the following is an example of a multicellular organism?**
   - (A) jellyfish
   - (B) bacterium
   - (C) amoeba
   - (D) paramecium

6. **In a multicellular organism, the cells __________ .**
   - (F) reproduce together
   - (G) grow to be the same size
   - (H) communicate with one another
   - (J) divide in the same amount of time

7. **The cell of a unicellular organism must be able to __________ .**
   - (A) make its own food
   - (B) convert sunlight into energy
   - (C) reproduce at least every hour
   - (D) get the nutrients the organism needs

STOP

Name____ Date____________________

Grade 6

Directions: Read the questions. Choose the truest possible answer.

1. **Cell division that produces new cells is called ________**

   (A) mitosis
   (B) osmosis
   (C) genetics
   (D) duplication

2. **Look at the cell below. Which picture shows what the result will be when the cell undergoes meiosis?**

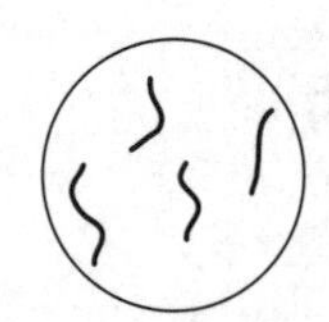

   (F)
   (G)
   (H)
   (J)

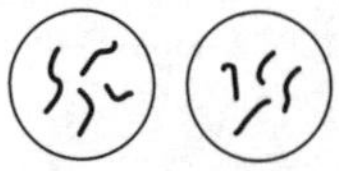

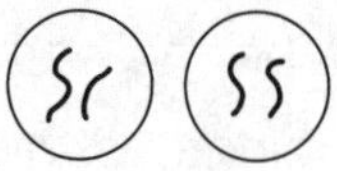

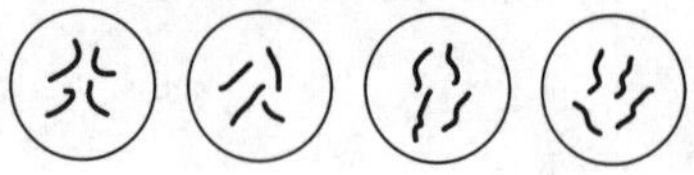

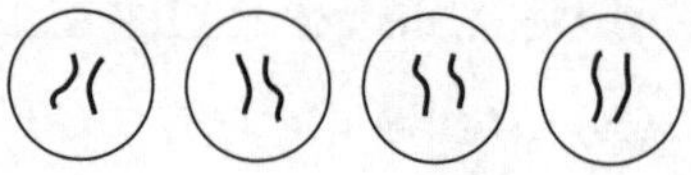

3. **What provides energy for cells to grow and divide?**

   (A) genes
   (B) nutrients
   (C) cytoplasm
   (D) chromosomes

4. **A new cell forms by mitosis from a cell that had ten chromosomes. How many chromosomes will the new cell have?**

   (F) 5
   (G) 10
   (H) 15
   (J) 20

5. **Which picture shows the result of mitosis in the cell below?**

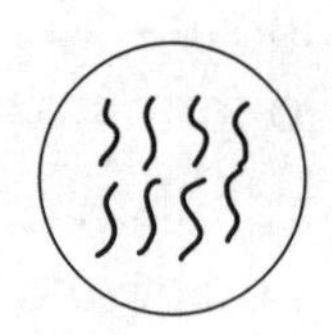

   (A)
   (B)
   (C)
   (D)

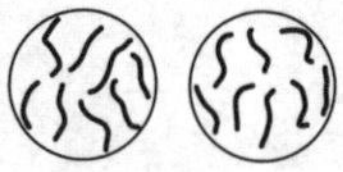

STOP

Name________________________________ Date________________

Grade 6

Directions: Read the questions. Choose the truest possible answer.

1. **Which of these is an example of a tissue in the human body?**
   - (A) lung
   - (B) liver
   - (C) tendon
   - (D) stomach

2. **Which of these tissues gives your body power and strength?**
   - (F) connective tissue
   - (G) skin tissue
   - (H) nerve tissue
   - (J) muscle tissue

3. **Nerve fibers send messages back and forth between the organs and muscles and the ________ .**
   - (A) brain
   - (B) bones
   - (C) skull
   - (D) tendons

4. **Cells in muscle tissue join together to form thousands of ________ .**
   - (F) fibers
   - (G) axons
   - (H) organs
   - (J) ligaments

Directions: Read each question. Write your answers on the lines provided.

5. **What is the function of skin tissue?**

____

6. **Explain why cells in heart tissue are different from cells in bone tissue.**

____

____

____

7. **Explain how muscle tissue works together to create movement in the body.**

____

____

____

STOP

Name________________________________ Date______________

Grade 6

Directions: Read the questions. Choose the truest possible answer.

1. **Organs are groups of specialized ________ .**
   - (A) cells
   - (B) fibers
   - (C) tissues
   - (D) systems

2. **Which organ is responsible for cleaning your blood?**
   - (F) liver
   - (G) kidney
   - (H) stomach
   - (J) intestine

3. **In which organ of your body will you find cardiac tissue?**
   - (A) liver
   - (B) heart
   - (C) lungs
   - (D) stomach

4. **What is the function of the stomach?**
   - (F) It filters out waste.
   - (G) It removes bacteria.
   - (H) It breaks down food.
   - (J) It separates liquids from solids.

5. **Which of the following is an organ in the human body?**
   - (A) skin
   - (B) socket
   - (C) ligament
   - (D) bicep

Directions: Read each question. Write your answers on the lines provided.

6. **What is the function of the lungs in the human body?**

____

____

____

7. **Identify and describe two functions of the brain.**

____

____

____

STOP

Name_______________________________ Date_______________

Grade 6

Directions: Read the questions. Choose the truest possible answer.

1. **Which of these is a communicable disease?**
   - (A) diabetes
   - (B) epilepsy
   - (C) influenza
   - (D) heart disease

2. **Disease can be caused by ________ .**
   - (F) saliva
   - (G) mucus
   - (H) viruses
   - (J) antibodies

3. **Jasper has diabetes. He accidentally sneezed on his friend Sayo. Sayo will not get diabetes from Jasper because diabetes is a ________ .**
   - (A) transferable disease
   - (B) communicable disease
   - (C) non-transferable disease
   - (D) non-communicable disease

4. **Tiny, one-celled organisms that can cause disease are ________ .**
   - (F) viruses
   - (G) bacteria
   - (H) mosses
   - (J) phagocytes

5. **White blood cells are part of the ________ system.**
   - (A) skeletal
   - (B) respiratory
   - (C) digestive
   - (D) immune

6. **Many diseases are not caused by infection but by ________ .**
   - (F) antibodies
   - (G) white blood cells
   - (H) antiserum in the bloodstream
   - (J) problems in structure or function

Directions: Read the question. Write your answers on the lines provided.

7. **Alice feels sick and goes to the doctor. The doctor prescribes an antibiotic. Several months later, Alice is sick again and goes to the doctor. This time, though, the doctor does not prescribe her an antibiotic. What are some possible reasons for this?**

____

____

____

STOP

Name____ Date____________________

Grade 6

Directions: Read each sentence below and fill in the blanks with words from the Word Bank.

Word Bank

roots	pistil	asexual reproduction	pollinate	gymnosperms
sugar	sperm	photosynthesis	stems	chloroplasts
pollen	fruit	chlorophyll	stamen	ovules

1. **In ____________________ , plants reproduce without sex cells.**

2. **The female reproductive organ of a flowering plant is the ____________________ .**

3. **____________________ is the green pigment plants use to capture energy from sunlight.**

4. **Sexual reproduction in plants involves an egg and a ____________________ .**

5. **Some plants rely on animals to ____________________ them by carrying pollen from flower to flower.**

6. **Some plants reproduce asexually when their ____________________ arch over and take root, forming new plants.**

7. **Non-flowering plants that produce seeds in cones are ____________________ .**

8. **Plant cells have ____________________ that contain chlorophyll.**

9. **A ____________________ is the male flower's reproductive organ.**

10. **A flower's egg cells develop in ____________________ .**

11. **In photosynthesis, carbon dioxide and water combine to produce oxygen and ____________________ .**

12. **The seeds of angiosperms are contained in ____________________ .**

13. **The sperm of flowering plants is contained in ____________________ , which is carried by the wind or animals to other plants.**

STOP

Name____ Date____________________

Grade 6

Directions: Read the questions. Choose the truest possible answer.

1. **Which process forms sex cells such as sperm and eggs?**
   - (A) mitosis
   - (B) meiosis
   - (C) asexual reproduction
   - (D) chromosomal reproduction

2. **Reproductive cells contain ________ as many chromosomes as their parent cell.**
   - (F) half
   - (G) twice
   - (H) exactly
   - (J) three times

3. **In asexual reproduction, how many parent cells are needed to make a new cell?**
   - (A) 1
   - (B) 2
   - (C) 3
   - (D) 4

4. **An egg that has been fertilized by a sperm forms a(n) ________ .**
   - (F) seed
   - (G) fetus
   - (H) zygote
   - (J) embryo

5. **Some organisms undergo a complete change from one form to another called ________ .**
   - (A) mitosis
   - (B) meiosis
   - (C) metabolism
   - (D) metamorphosis

6. **Which shows the basic life cycle of most animals from beginning to end?**
   - (F) reproduction → birth → growth → death
   - (G) birth → growth → reproduction → death
   - (H) growth → reproduction → birth → death
   - (J) birth → reproduction → growth → death

7. **What happens when a sperm cell joins with an egg cell?**
   - (A) adaptation
   - (B) fertilization
   - (C) hibernation
   - (D) reproduction

STOP

Name______________________________ Date______________

Grade 6

Directions: Read each question. Write your answers on the lines provided.

1. **There are two human systems that contain different components depending on whether the individual is male or female. They are the reproductive system and the ________ system.**
   - (A) respiratory
   - (B) circulatory
   - (C) endocrine
   - (D) digestive

2. **In the endocrine system, chemicals called ________ are released, which help control the activities of the individual.**
   - (F) hormones
   - (G) antibodies
   - (H) enzymes
   - (J) impulses

Directions: Read each question. Write your answers on the lines provided.

3. **How do the muscular and skeletal systems work together in your body?**

____

____

____

4. **Describe how the respiratory and circulatory systems work together to get oxygen to cells. Be sure to describe the job of each organ involved.**

____

____

____

____

____

____

____

STOP

0-7696-8066-6—*Science Test Practice*

Name_______________________________ Date_______________

Grade 6

Directions: Read the questions. Choose the truest possible answer.

1. **The passage of genetic information from one generation to another is called ________ .**
   - (A) mitosis
   - (B) meiosis
   - (C) heredity
   - (D) osmosis

2. **Where in a cell are genes found?**
   - (F) the nucleus
   - (G) the vacuole
   - (H) the chloroplast
   - (J) the mitochondrion

3. **Genes occupy specific locations on ________ .**
   - (A) cilia
   - (B) flagella
   - (C) ribosomes
   - (D) chromosomes

4. **Genes contain ________ .**
   - (F) DNA
   - (G) ribosomes
   - (H) chromosomes
   - (J) mitochondrion

5. **How many different genes can a human cell have?**
   - (A) one
   - (B) ten
   - (C) hundreds
   - (D) thousands

6. **Genes control the structure and function of ________ .**
   - (F) the brain only
   - (G) the entire organism
   - (H) the entire circulatory system
   - (J) the skeletal system

7. **How many of its genes does each offspring receive from its father?**
   - (A) all
   - (B) half
   - (C) one quarter
   - (D) three quarters

GO ON

Name________________________________ Date______________

Grade 6

Directions: Read the questions. Choose the truest possible answer.

1. **How many copies of each gene does a human body cell have?**
   - (A) 1
   - (B) 2
   - (C) 3
   - (D) 4

2. **A gene that determines the trait that is shown in an offspring is called _________ .**
   - (F) dominant
   - (G) assertive
   - (H) recessive
   - (J) reproductive

3. **The gene that does *not* determine the trait you see in an offspring is called _________ .**
   - (A) leading
   - (B) reserved
   - (C) dominant
   - (D) recessive

Directions: Read the text below. Use information from the text to help you answer question 4.

In humans, the gene for brown eyes is dominant, and the gene for blue eyes is recessive. The mother in a family has brown eyes. She has two copies of the dominant gene for brown eyes. The father also has brown eyes. He has one copy of the dominant gene for brown eyes and one copy of the recessive gene for blue eyes.

4. **Complete the Punnett square to show the genes of the parents and the possible combinations of genes for eye color in their offspring. Use B for brown and b for blue.**

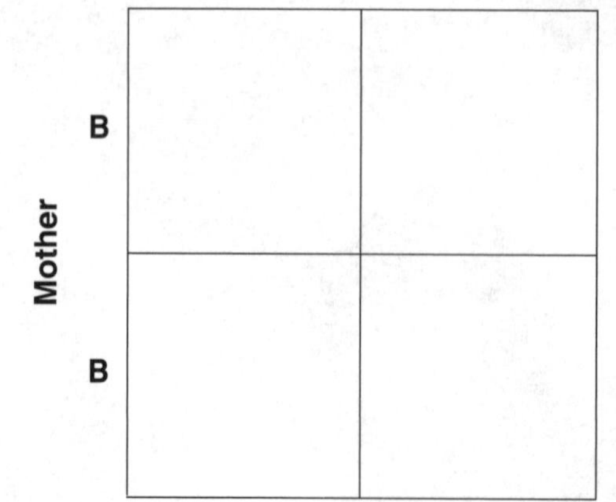

STOP

Name______________________ Date______________

Grade 6

Directions: Read each question. Write your answer on the lines provided.

1. **How is an inherited trait different from a learned behavior?**

2. **Describe an inherited trait that you received from your parents. Explain how you know it is an inherited trait and not a learned behavior.**

3. **Imagine you are eating dinner with your family. You use a fork to put a piece of food in your mouth. Then you chew your food and swallow it. Which of these actions is an instinctual behavior, and which is a learned behavior? Explain.**

4. **Give an example of a learned behavior you have and how you developed that behavior.**

STOP

Name________________________________ Date________________

Grade 6

Directions: Read the following passage and fill in the blanks with words from the Word Bank. Some words will be used more than once.

Word Bank

ecosystem	environment	habitat	niche	abiotic	community
population	biotic	producers	consumers	decomposers	sunlight

All living things have needs. In order to survive, living organisms need air to breathe, water to drink, food to eat, and a place to live. The surroundings in which an organism lives is called the **1.** ________________ . Here, the organism is provided with all the specific things it requires to survive.

An environment is made up of living, or **2.** ________________ , and non-living, or **3.** ________________ parts. Living parts of the environment include all of the organisms there. Non-living parts include soil, water, and air, as well as other things like the weather and temperature. The part of an environment in which an organism lives in is called its **4.** ________________ .

Organisms of the same species living in the same environment at the same time make up a **5.** ________________, like all the people living in your town or city. Many of these groups living together in the same environment make up a **6.** ________________ . Here, organisms interact with each other. **7.** ________________ may cause a dead tree to decay, which provides nutrients for the soil.

An **8.** ________________ is made up of a community and all of the non-living parts of its environment. The main source of energy for an ecosystem is **9.** ________________ . This source provides energy for **10.** ________________ to make their own food. Plants provide food for organisms that are **11.** ________________ and cannot make their own food.

Every organism has a specific role in an ecosystem. This is called its **12.** ________________ . This includes everything an organism does and everything it needs.

Name________________________ Date____________

Grade 6

Directions: Identify each of the following organisms as a producer, consumer, or decomposer.

1\.

____

2\.

____

3\.

____

4\.

____

5\.

____

6\.

____

7\.

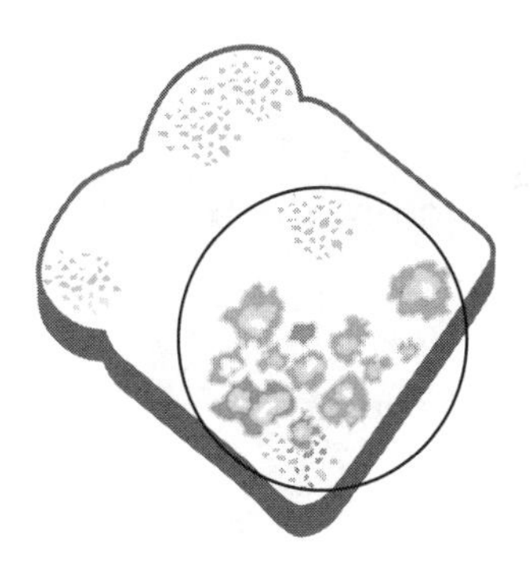

____

8\.

____

STOP

Name______________________________ Date______________

Grade 6

Directions: Study the food web below. Use information from the food web to help you answer questions 1–3.

A food web shows the flow of energy in an ecosystem. Each arrow points from an organism to one of its possible predators.

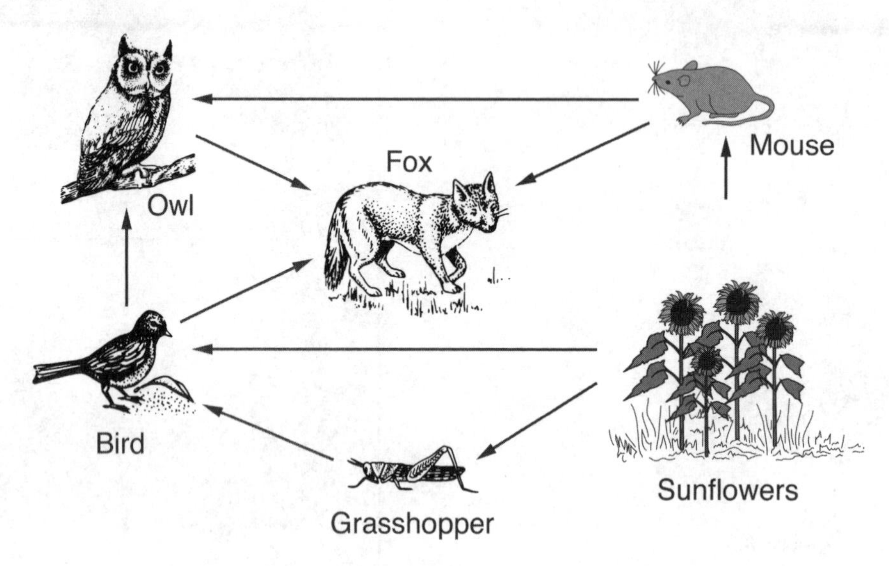

1. **What do the arrows in the food web represent?**

____

____

2. **Which organism is the producer in the food web, and which organisms eat this producer?**

____

____

____

3. **Describe a situation in the food web in which two organisms are competing for the same food.**

____

____

____

STOP

Name________________________ Date____________

Grade 6

Directions: Study the graphs below. Use the information from the graphs to help you answer questions 1–4.

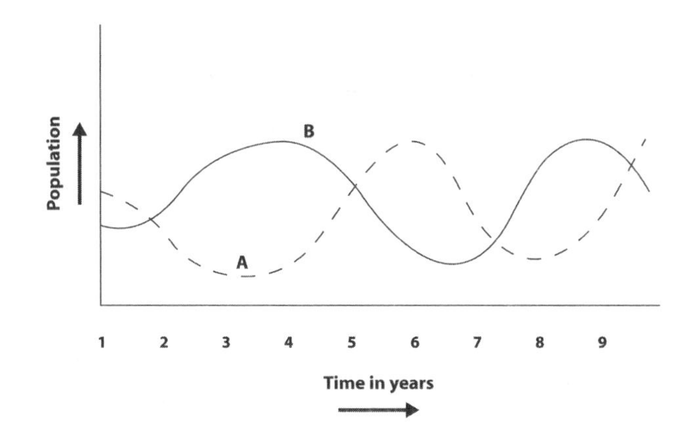

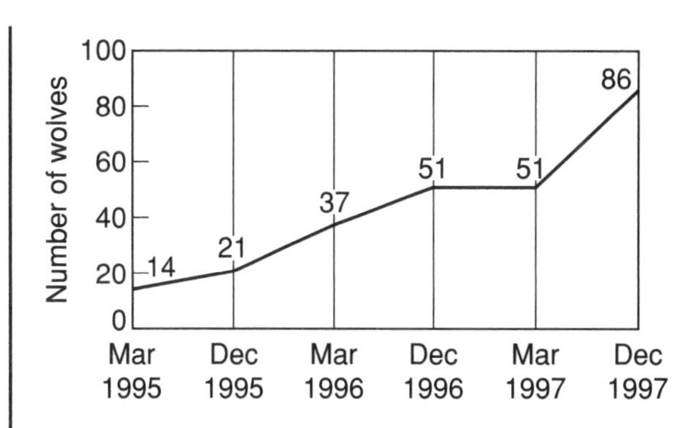

1. **Suppose line B on the graph shows a population of mice. What does line A show?**
   - Ⓐ the population of a seed-bearing plant that the mice eat
   - Ⓑ the population of a predator of the mice
   - Ⓒ the number of possible offspring a mouse can have
   - Ⓓ the number of appropriate nesting sites

2. **At what time is there probably the most food available for the mice?**
   - Ⓕ between years 1 and 2
   - Ⓖ between years 3 and 4
   - Ⓗ between years 5 and 6
   - Ⓙ between years 6 and 7

3. **In 1995, 14 wolves were brought into the Greater Yellowstone area. The graph shows the changes in the wolf population since that time. During which time period did the population change the most?**
   - Ⓐ March 1995 to December 1995
   - Ⓑ December 1995 to March 1996
   - Ⓒ March 1996 to December 1996
   - Ⓓ March 1997 to December 1997

4. **What happened between December 1996 and March 1997?**
   - Ⓕ the number of wolves born equaled the number of wolves that died
   - Ⓖ the number of wolves born exceeded the number of wolves that died
   - Ⓗ the number of wolves that died was less than the number of wolves that were born
   - Ⓙ the number of wolves that died exceeded the number of wolves that were born

Name____ Date__________________

Grade 6

Directions: Read the questions. Choose the truest possible answer.

1. Which of the following is an herbivore?

- (A) hawk
- (B) mouse
- (C) snake
- (D) spider

2. Which of the following is a predator of mice?

- (F) toad
- (G) snake
- (H) spider
- (J) grasshopper

3. In which food chain is the most energy lost from the ecosystem?

- (A) plants → birds → snakes
- (B) plants → herbivorous insects → spiders → carnivorous insects
- (C) plants → herbivorous insects → carnivorous insects → birds
- (D) plants → herbivorous insects → carnivorous insects → spiders → insect-eating birds

4. How does a decomposer get energy?

- (F) by making its own food
- (G) by eating live plants
- (H) by eating live animals
- (J) by breaking down the remains of dead organisms

5. An organism that grows, feeds, and is sheltered on or in another organism is __________ .

- (A) a predator
- (B) a prey
- (C) a parasite
- (D) a host

6. Which of the following would probably cause an increase in the snake population of a forest?

- (F) an increase in the population of owls
- (G) an increase in the population of mice
- (H) a decrease in the population of fish
- (J) a decrease in the population of insects

7 An organism's niche is __________ .

- (A) its preferred habitat
- (B) its main source of food
- (C) its role in an ecosystem
- (D) the predators that depend on it

STOP

Name______________________________ Date______________

Grade 6

Directions: Read the text below. Use information from the text to help you answer the essay question. Use a separate sheet of paper if needed.

Your Best Defense

Take a look around you. Pollen fills the air, germs cover every surface, and smog clogs the sky. The world is full of sicknesses that are waiting to happen. With bacteria and viruses seemingly everywhere, how does the human body have a chance of defending itself? Luckily, people have a built-in system that is constantly fighting off these invaders. This system is called the immune system.

The immune system's first line of defense is hard to miss. When a harmful bacteria or virus, also called a pathogen, tries to invade your body, it must first get through your skin. Skin acts like a protective wall. It is made of layers of flat cells. The outer layers of skin are dead cells. This keeps the pathogens from finding a living cell to infect. Over time, the dead cells flake off, taking the pathogens along with them. New dead skin cells replace the old ones.

What happens if a pathogen breaks through this protective wall of skin? This can happen if a person has a cut, even if it is not visible. Have you ever wondered why you bleed when you get cut? This reaction is all part of the body's defenses. Blood flows to open cuts because the body is trying to keep pathogens out! Inside the blood are small cell parts called platelets. Platelets come together to seal off an open wound—not to make you feel better, but to keep out harmful pathogens.

Once a pathogen enters the body, the real battle begins. The immune system hurries into action, releasing special cells that have no other purpose but to fight pathogens. These cells perform a variety of functions, each with its own job. Some cells move in to identify the pathogen so other cells can attack and kill it. There are even cells that remember how the body stopped different pathogens. So in the future, if you get sick from a pathogen you've had before, your body will be able to beat it faster!

1. **Using information from the passage and your knowledge of science, explain why it is important in today's world to have a strong immune system.**

____

____

____

____

____

____

STOP

0-7696-8066-6—*Science Test Practice*

Name________________________ Date____________

Grade 6

Directions: Read the questions. Choose the truest possible answer.

1. **Hygiene is the science of**
   - Ⓐ addictive behavior.
   - Ⓑ preserving your health.
   - Ⓒ nutrients that are needed by the body.
   - Ⓓ the body's overreaction to common substances.

2. **What is the best way to prevent the spread of disease?**
   - Ⓕ exercising regularly
   - Ⓖ washing your hands
   - Ⓗ flossing your teeth daily
   - Ⓙ developing good posture

3. **Which of these increases the heart rate and helps distribute oxygen throughout the body?**
   - Ⓐ obesity
   - Ⓑ deep sleep
   - Ⓒ aerobic exercise
   - Ⓓ the immune system

4. **How many hours of sleep are recommended for young people?**
   - Ⓕ about 6
   - Ⓖ about 9
   - Ⓗ about 12
   - Ⓙ more than 12

5. **Obesity can increase the risk of which health problem?**
   - Ⓐ diabetes
   - Ⓑ heart disease
   - Ⓒ high blood pressure
   - Ⓓ all of the above

6. **Which statement about regular exercise is false?**
   - Ⓕ Exercise burns calories.
   - Ⓖ Exercise conserves nutrients.
   - Ⓗ Exercise increases the effects of stress.
   - Ⓙ Exercise strengthens the heart, lungs, and bones.

Directions: Read the question. Write your answer on the lines provided.

7. **Why are brushing and flossing important to keeping your teeth healthy?**

____

____

____

____

____

____

STOP

Name ____________________ Date ____________

Grade 6

Directions: Read the questions. Choose the truest possible answers.

1. **__________ measure the energy in the food you eat.**
   - (A) Fats
   - (B) Calories
   - (C) Minerals
   - (D) Food pyramids

2. **Nutrients serve what purpose in the human body?**
   - (F) They prevent injury.
   - (G) They distribute oxygen.
   - (H) They act as the first line of defense.
   - (J) They provide materials needed for life.

3. **The number of calories a person needs can depend on __________, __________, and __________.**
   - (A) age, size, appearance
   - (B) size, sex, physical activity
   - (C) sex, age, members of your family
   - (D) diet, intelligence, physical activity

4. **What percentage of your body is made up of water?**
   - (F) less than 1%
   - (G) 20%
   - (H) 50%
   - (J) 70%

5. **Which is *not* one of the functions of water in the human body?**
   - (A) to store energy
   - (B) to make body liquids more fluid
   - (C) to move substances around
   - (D) to control body temperature

6. **What is the best way to eat healthy?**
   - (F) Always eat as many calories as possible.
   - (G) Find one healthy food that you like and eat it all the time.
   - (H) Try to balance your diet by eating a variety of healthy foods.
   - (J) Only eat foods that you enjoy eating, and eat them whenever you want.

Directions: Read the question. Write your answer on the lines provided.

7. **List the six food groups recommended for healthy eating.**

   ____

   ____

   ____

Name______________________________ Date______________

Grade 6

Directions: Study the diagram below. Use information from the diagram to help you answer questions 1–2.

The plant above was recently placed next to the light source.

1. **In which direction will the plant grow?**
   - Ⓐ upward
   - Ⓑ to the right
   - Ⓒ downward
   - Ⓓ to the left

2. **To which outside stimuli will the roots respond?**
   - Ⓕ light and water
   - Ⓖ water and gravity
   - Ⓗ light and gravity
   - Ⓙ light, gravity, and water

Directions: Study the diagrams below. Use information from the diagrams to help you answer question 3.

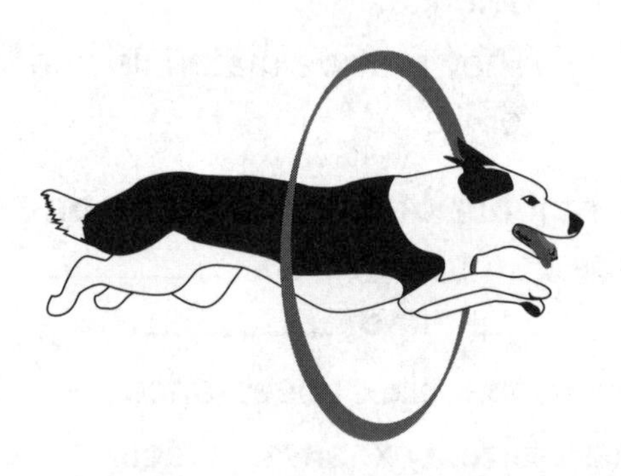

3. **Which diagram above represents an instinctive behavior? Why?**

____

____

____

____

STOP

0-7696-8066-6—*Science Test Practice*

Name________________________________ Date________________

Grade 6

Directions: Read the text below. Use information from the text to help you answer the question.

Arctic Adaptations

The Arctic is a region of Earth near the North Pole. The Arctic has extremely cold temperatures and harsh conditions. As a result of the cold environment, animals in the Arctic have various adaptations to help them survive.

The arctic fox changes color. In summer, the arctic fox's fur is gray. In winter, the fur thickens and turns white, camouflaging the animal against the snow. To reduce heat loss, the arctic fox has a short nose and legs, a bushy tail, and small ears. It has thick fur with hollow hairs that trap its body heat. Its feet are covered with fur, so it can run easily across the snow.

The caribou is a large, elk-like herbivore that lives in large herds. Caribou herds migrate long distances in search of food. The calves are able to run soon after they are born, which allows them to keep up with the constantly moving herds. A caribou's hairs are hollow and trap air. This helps to keep the animal warm and helps it stay afloat when swimming.

The ptarmigan is a bird that is brown in summer and white in winter, allowing it to blend into the changing tundra landscape. Although ptarmigans can fly, they generally walk from plant to plant, eating berries and leaves. Feathers on ptarmigans' feet act like snowshoes, so the birds can walk on snow without sinking in. Ptarmigans have a thick layer of tiny down feathers that keeps them warm.

1. **Using information from the passage and your knowledge of science, explain why it is necessary for animals to adapt to their surroundings.**

____

____

____

____

____

____

____

____

____

____ STOP

0-7696-8066-6—*Science Test Practice*

Name____ Date________________

Grade 6

Directions: Read the text below. Use information from the text to help you answer questions 1–3.

Desert Plants

In a desert, little rain falls, and daytime temperatures are generally high. Yet many plants live in deserts. They have adaptations that help them survive in this environment.

Some plants, such as the mesquite tree, have very long roots that extend deep into the ground. These roots draw water from a deep underground supply.

Other desert plants, such as the saguaro cactus, are able to store water. Because roots of the saguaro cactus grow only a few centimeters deep, it cannot draw much water from underground. However, this plant can absorb a large amount of water after a rain and store it in its stems. Some plants, such as the Joshua tree, have a waxy covering on their leaves that keeps water in.

Slow growth, which conserves food, energy, and water, is another adaptation of desert plants. Some plants, such as the acacia tree, maintain slow growth by losing their leaves during long dry spells. Without leaves, the plant loses far less water through evaporation and also conserves food, water, and energy.

Other plants, such as the Desert Paintbrush, survive the harsh conditions by having a short life cycle. After the winter rains, they grow quickly, flower, and die, scattering their seeds on the desert floor. The following spring, the seeds germinate and the cycle repeats.

1. **What is the main problem desert plants face?**

____

____

2. **The leaves of a maple tree have many small openings in them. Water vapor and other gases pass in and out of the plant through these openings. Could the maple tree survive in a desert? Why or why not?**

____

____

3. **Why is a short life cycle a good adaptation to desert conditions?**

____

____

STOP

Name________________________________ Date________________

Grade 6

Directions: Read the text below. Use information from the text to help you answer the essay question. Use a separate sheet of paper if needed.

Extinction

Many species that once lived on Earth are extinct, or no longer living. Extinction is caused by both natural disasters and human activities.

Scientists hypothesize that a mass extinction occurred 65 million years ago. They believe that the extinction was caused when a giant asteroid struck Earth. Among the species destroyed during the extinction were dinosaurs.

Today, the Florida panther is an endangered species, which means it is in danger of becoming extinct. The Florida panther needs a large area to hunt and survive. Destruction of wilderness areas and illegal hunting have dramatically reduced the number of Florida panthers.

1. **In the last few centuries, the number of species becoming extinct has increased significantly. Currently, there are nearly 400 animals on the endangered species list. Using your knowledge of science, explain why this is most likely the case. Consider how human activities contribute to the extinction of a species.**

____

____

____

____

____

____

____

____

____

____

____

____

____

STOP

Name________________________ Date____________

Grade 6

Directions: Read the text below. Use information from the passage to help you answer questions 1–3.

Fossilization

A fossil is the remains of an animal or plant preserved from an earlier era. The fossilized remains of animals are usually found inside rocks. A fossil may be a footprint, a cast of the inside of the organism, or an impression of the outside of the organism. The process of fossil formation is known as fossilization.

Fossilization often begins when an aquatic animal dies and sinks to the floor of a sea or a lake. If it is not eaten, it is eventually buried under sand and dirt. Gradually, the soft body parts decay, but the hard parts may be preserved. Over a long period of time, more layers of sediment build up. After millions of years, these sediments turn into sedimentary rock. The animal's remains that are preserved within the rock become fossilized.

In a few cases, fossils are preserved intact. For example, in Siberia scientists uncovered the remains of a nearly intact woolly mammoth. After the creature died, its remains were frozen in a block of ice. Today scientists continue to study the woolly mammoth in order to learn more about the time in which it lived.

1. **Why does it take millions of years for most fossils to form?**

____

____

2. **What can you infer about the steps in the formation of the woolly mammoth fossils?**

____

____

____

____

3. **Many of the fossils that scientists find are from extinct plants and animals. Explain two things scientists can learn by studying these fossils.**

____

____

____

STOP

Name____________________ Date__________

Grade 6

Directions: Each number in the diagram below represents a layer of Earth. Complete 1–6 by filling in the name of the correct layer.

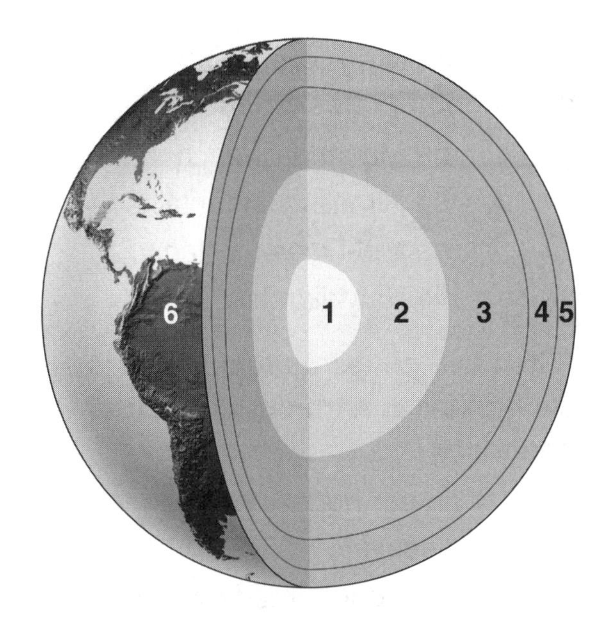

1. ____________________
2. ____________________
3. ____________________
4. ____________________
5. ____________________
6. ____________________

Directions: Complete the following items by filling in the blanks.

7. **The __________ is a layer of rock about 30 kilometers thick.**
8. **The __________ is the hottest layer of Earth and is hotter than the surface of the sun.**
9. **The __________ is a constantly moving liquid made up mainly of iron and nickel.**
10. **The __________ includes all of the crust and part of the upper mantle, and it rests on the asthenosphere.**

STOP

Name______________________________ Date______________

Grade 6

Directions: Study the diagram below. Use the diagram to help you answer questions 1–2.

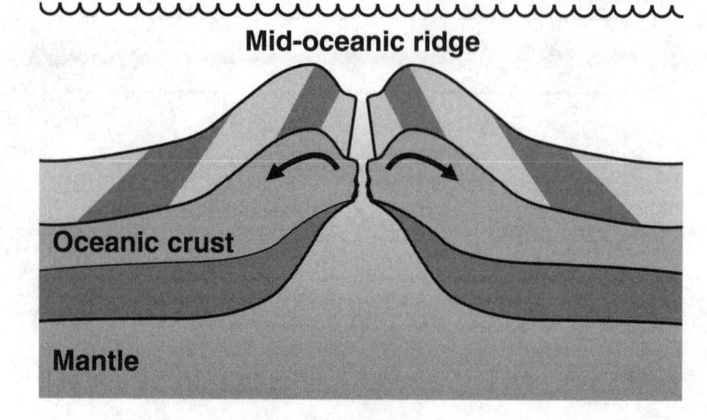

1. **This is an example of a ________ .**
   - Ⓐ convergent boundary
   - Ⓑ divergent boundary
   - Ⓒ transform-fault boundary
   - Ⓓ subduction zone

2. **Which of these describes what is happening in the diagram?**
   - Ⓕ Both plates grind past each other.
   - Ⓖ One plate sinks beneath the other.
   - Ⓗ The plates are moving toward each other.
   - Ⓙ The plates are moving away from each other.

Directions: Read the questions. Choose the truest possible answer.

3. **Which landform was created when two continental plates collided?**
   - Ⓐ the Marianas Trench
   - Ⓑ the Himalaya Mountains
   - Ⓒ the Mid-Ocean Ridge
   - Ⓓ the Hawaiian Islands

4. **When two plates suddenly slip past each other at a transform-fault boundary, ________ .**
   - Ⓕ an earthquake occurs
   - Ⓖ a volcano occurs
   - Ⓗ sea-floor spreading takes place
   - Ⓙ subduction occurs

5. **What is the Ring of Fire?**
   - Ⓐ a line of volcanoes and earthquakes around the Pacific Ocean
   - Ⓑ the use of heat from a volcano as a source of energy
   - Ⓒ the center of a volcano
   - Ⓓ an explosive volcano eruption

STOP

Name____________________ Date__________

Grade 6

Directions: Study the diagram below. Use information from the diagram to help you answer questions 1–4.

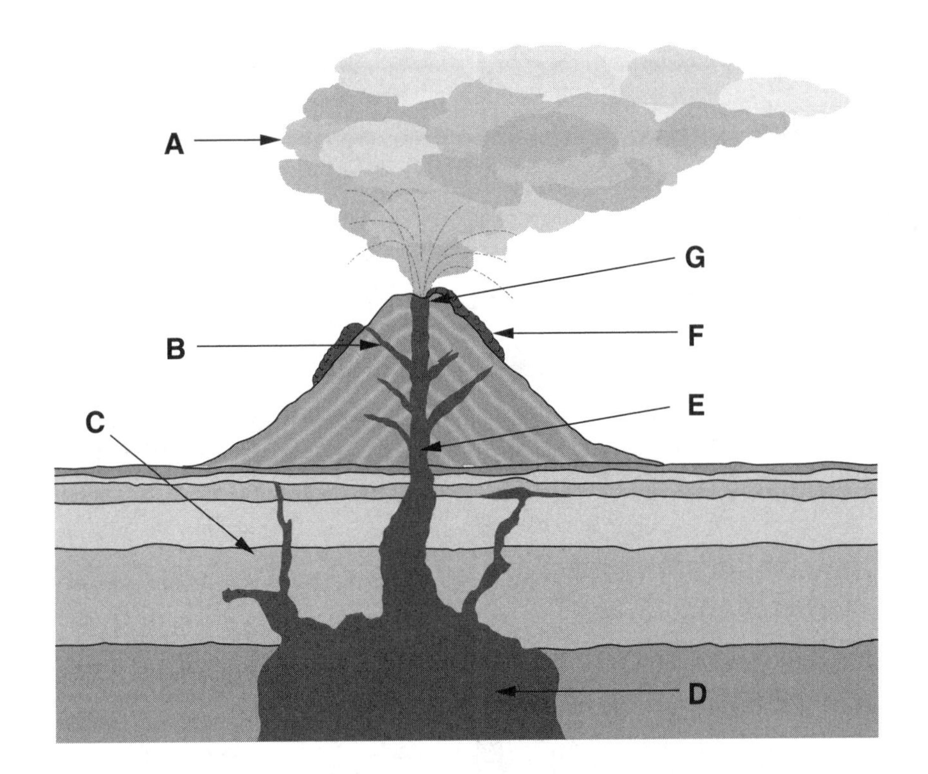

1. **A huge underground storage area of molten rock is located at "D." This is the __________ .**
   - Ⓐ crater
   - Ⓑ magma chamber
   - Ⓒ vent
   - Ⓓ lava

2. **If "F" is always released from a volcano, a __________ .**
   - Ⓕ cinder volcano will form
   - Ⓖ composite volcano will form
   - Ⓗ shield volcano will form
   - Ⓙ steep-sided volcano will form

3. **What happens if "E" becomes blocked?**
   - Ⓐ Lava flows slowly out of the volcano.
   - Ⓑ Pressure builds up and an explosive eruption occurs.
   - Ⓒ Magma turns into hot gas.
   - Ⓓ Magma drains back into the earth.

4. **"A" generally contains __________ .**
   - Ⓕ lava
   - Ⓖ magma and gas
   - Ⓗ dust
   - Ⓙ steam, gas, and dust

Name_______________________________ Date_______________

Grade 6

Directions: Read each question. Write your answers on the lines provided.

1. **How does the tree above act as an agent for weathering? Explain.**

____

____

____

____

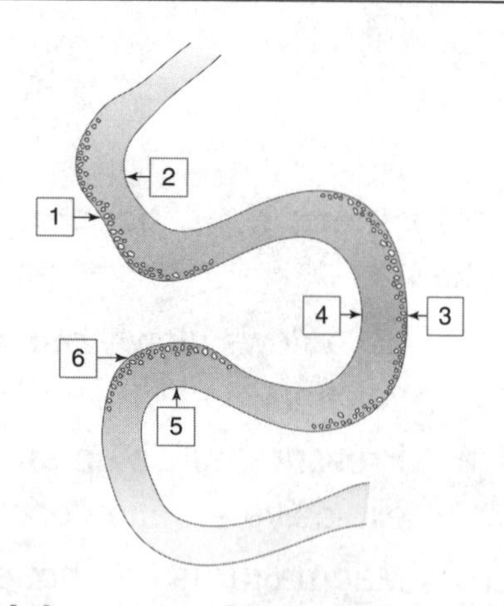

2. **In which areas of the diagram above will erosion of the riverbank occur? Why?**

____

____

____

____

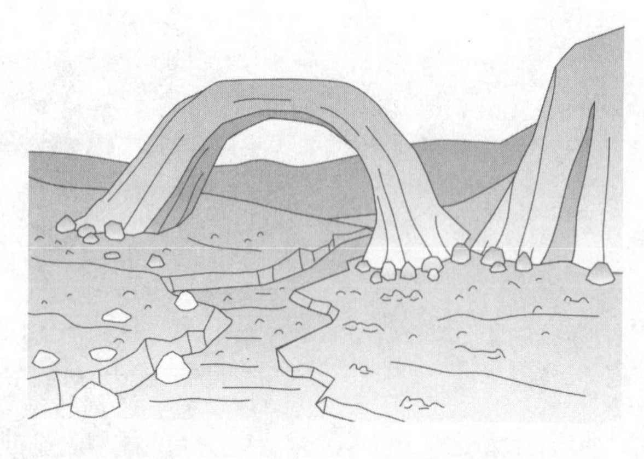

3. **How did erosion form the landform above?**

____

____

____

____

4. **How do temperature changes cause weathering?**

____

____

____

____

____

____

STOP

Name_______________________________ Date_______________

Grade 6

Directions: Use the words in the Word Bank to fill in the diagram of the rock cycle.

Word Bank

melting	metamorphic rocks	sediments
deposition	sedimentary rocks	igneous rocks

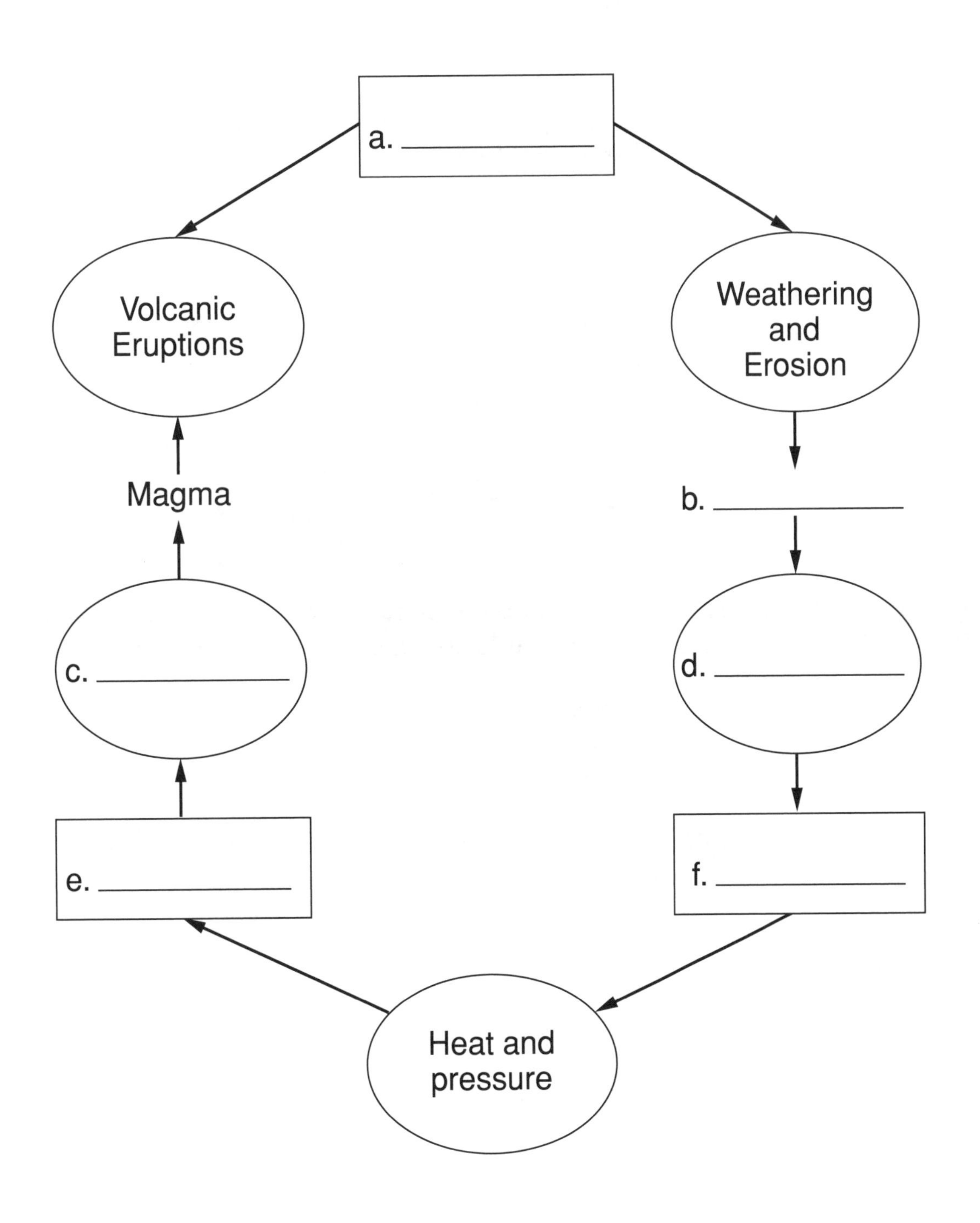

STOP

Name________________________________ Date______________

Grade 6

Directions: Study the chart below. Use the chart to help you answer the question.

Some Methods of Protecting Soil

Method	What is done	How it helps
Contour-plowing	plowing the field along the side of a hill rather than up and down	prvents water from running downhill and reduces erosion
Debris dams	building dams in steep gullies from tree stumps, branches, and other organic matter	slows water running down a hill and reduces erosion
Reduced tillage	plowing only areas that must be plowed	disturbs soil as little as possible and leaves vegetation to hold the soil in place
Retirement fencing	fencing in areas where the soil has been eroded to prevent grazing	allows vegetation to grow back; often trees are planted to help hold the soil in place
Riparian fencing	building fences and planting trees along rivers and streams	prevents cattle from trampling riverbanks so natural vegetation can grow back and hold soil in place
Strip-cropping	alternating different crops in strips along the side of a hill	prevents water from running downhill; any nutrients that run off of one section are caught by the next section
Stubble-mulching	leaving the stubs and plants in a field	keeps soil covered, reduces evaporation, and catches snow in winter; also enriches the soil
Terracing	building flat terraces on steep hills	allows no runoff; can reduce erosion to 1/20 of what it otherwise would be

1. Choose any two of the soil conservation methods listed in the chart above, and draw pictures that clearly portray the methods you chose. Be sure to label important features of each picture.

STOP

Name ______________________________ Date ______________

Grade 6

Directions: Study the diagram below. Use it to help you answer questions 1–3.

1. **Compare and contrast what happens at points A and D.**

____

____

2. **What process takes place at point B and what is the result?**

____

____

3. **How much of the water used in the water cycle returns to the cycle to be used again?**
   - (A) 25%
   - (B) 50%
   - (C) 75%
   - (D) 100%

Directions: Read the question. Write your answer on the lines provided.

4. **Fresh water is renewed through the water cycle, but people must still conserve water. Give two reasons why.**

____

____

____

____

______________________________ STOP

0-7696-8066-6—*Science Test Practice*

Name________________________________ Date______________

Grade 6

Directions: Read the following passage and fill in the blanks with words from the Word Bank.

Word Bank

atmosphere	exosphere	helium	mesosphere	ozone
space	stratosphere	temperature	thermosphere	troposphere

Earth is surrounded by a blanket of air known as the **1.** __________ , which contains distinct layers. These layers vary in **2.** __________ , composition, and density.

The first layer, the **3.** __________ , which is closest to Earth, contains about three-quarters of the total mass of the atmosphere. Climate and weather also occur in this layer, which is the densest layer.

The second layer, the **4.** __________ , begins between 8 and 14.5 kilometers above Earth's surface, and extends to 50 kilometers above the surface. This layer contains the **5.** __________ , which absorbs and scatters ultraviolet radiation from the sun.

The third layer extends to 85 kilometers high. In this layer, the **6.** __________ , temperatures drop to as low as -93 degrees Celsius. In the fourth layer, the **7.** __________ , temperatures rise again and may reach 1,727 degrees Celsius. This layer, where manmade satellites orbit, extends to 600 kilometers above Earth. Beyond this layer is the **8.** __________ . It continues until it merges with **9.** __________ , where the main gases are hydrogen and **10.** __________ .

Directions: Read the questions. Choose the truest possible answer.

11. When a warm air mass meets a cold air mass, the __________ .

- (A) cold and warm air mix
- (B) warm air sinks below the cold air
- (C) cold air sinks below the warm air
- (D) cold air and warm air push against each other

12. Air pressure is measured with a __________ .

- (F) hygrometer
- (G) barometer
- (H) thermometer
- (J) seismometer

Name____________________ Date__________

Grade 6

Directions: Using words from the Word Bank, label the cloud diagrams below.

Word Bank

cumulus	cumulonimbus	cirrus	stratus	cirrocumulus

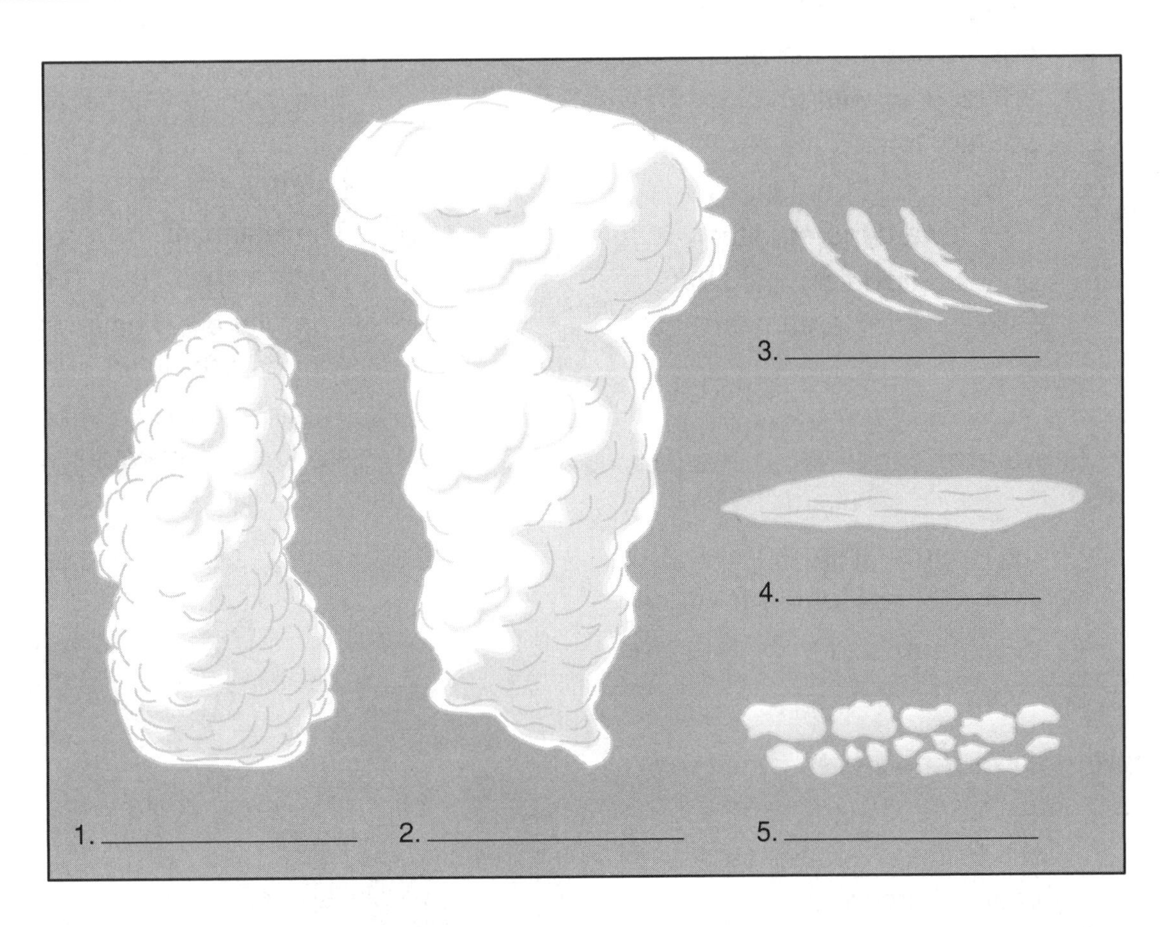

Directions: Read each question. Write your answers on the lines provided.

6. Compare and contrast cirrus clouds and cumulus clouds.

____

____

7. Leanna hears on the news that there will be thunderstorms in a few hours. She then steps outside, and notices high, thin cirrus clouds in the sky. Is Leanna's observation of cirrus clouds consistent with the weather forecast? Why or why not?

____

____

Name____ Date____________________

Grade 6

Directions: Read the questions. Choose the truest possible answer.

1. **The Gulf Stream affects climate by ________ .**

   Ⓐ bringing warmth from the equator toward the South Pole
   Ⓑ bringing warmth from the equator toward the North Pole
   Ⓒ bringing cold from the South Pole toward the equator
   Ⓓ bringing cold from the North Pole toward the equator

2. **Where are hurricanes most likely to form?**

   Ⓕ over warm ocean water
   Ⓖ over cold ocean water
   Ⓗ over warm land
   Ⓙ over cold land

3. **During an El Niño weather pattern, ________ .**

   Ⓐ winds in the Pacific Ocean change direction
   Ⓑ warm water is pushed westward toward Australia and Southeast Asia
   Ⓒ fewer storms occur along the west coasts of North and South America
   Ⓓ the Atlantic Ocean waters become warmer

4. **How would an island's climate compare to the climate of a land-locked country, if both are at the same latitude?**

   Ⓕ The island will have the same climate as the land-locked country.
   Ⓖ The island will have warmer winters and cooler summers.
   Ⓗ The island will have warmer winters and hotter summers.
   Ⓙ The island will have cooler summers and colder winters.

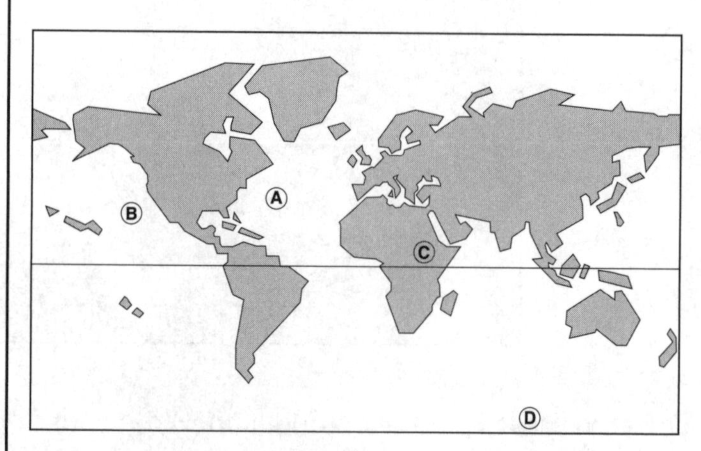

5. **Look at the diagram above. Which letter indicates the location of the Gulf Stream?**

   Ⓐ A
   Ⓑ B
   Ⓒ C
   Ⓓ D

STOP

Name ______________________ Date ______________

Grade 6

Directions: Study the diagram of the solar system below. Complete the diagram by filling in the names of the planetary objects.

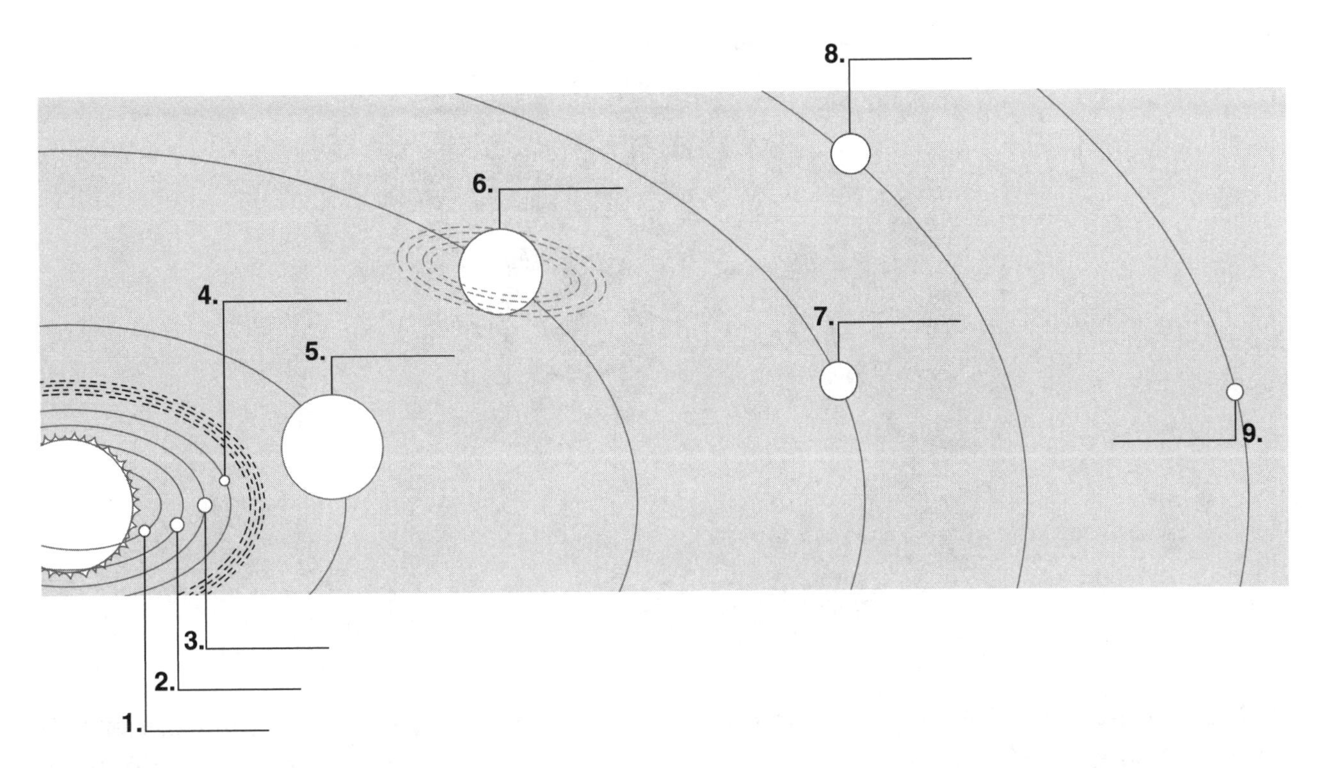

10. Name four other objects found in our solar system that are *not* shown in the diagram.

____

____

____

____

Name____ Date______________

Grade 6

Directions: Study the diagram below. Use information from the diagram to help you answer questions 1–5.

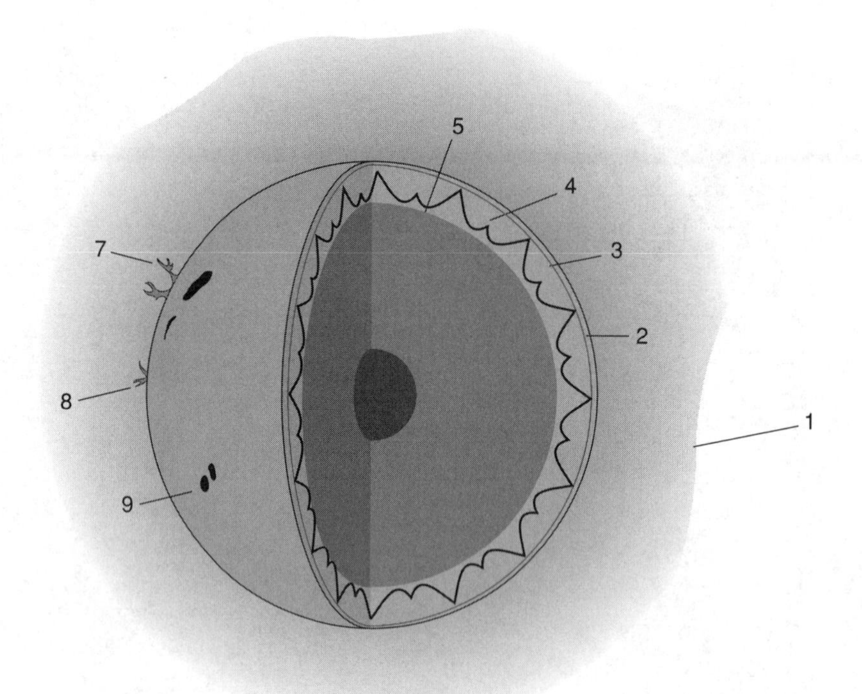

1. **Which number on the diagram shows the hottest part of the sun?**
   - Ⓐ 5
   - Ⓑ 6
   - Ⓒ 7
   - Ⓓ 8

2. **Number 2 in the diagram represents the __________ .**
   - Ⓕ corona
   - Ⓖ prominence
   - Ⓗ chromosphere
   - Ⓙ convective zone

3. **What does number 9 represent in the diagram?**
   - Ⓐ sunspot
   - Ⓑ radiance
   - Ⓒ solar flare
   - Ⓓ prominence

4. **Which number on the diagram shows the part of the sun you can see during a total eclipse?**
   - Ⓕ 1
   - Ⓖ 3
   - Ⓗ 5
   - Ⓙ 6

5. **The sunlight that reaches Earth comes from number 3, which is called the __________ .**
   - Ⓐ photosphere
   - Ⓑ corona
   - Ⓒ chromosphere
   - Ⓓ solar flare

STOP

Name____ Date________________

Grade 6

Directions: Read the questions. Choose the truest possible answer.

1. **What is a galaxy?**
   - Ⓐ a group of planets
   - Ⓑ a large system of stars
   - Ⓒ a system of galactic clusters
   - Ⓓ a group of stars that forms a shape

2. **What type of galaxy is shown?**

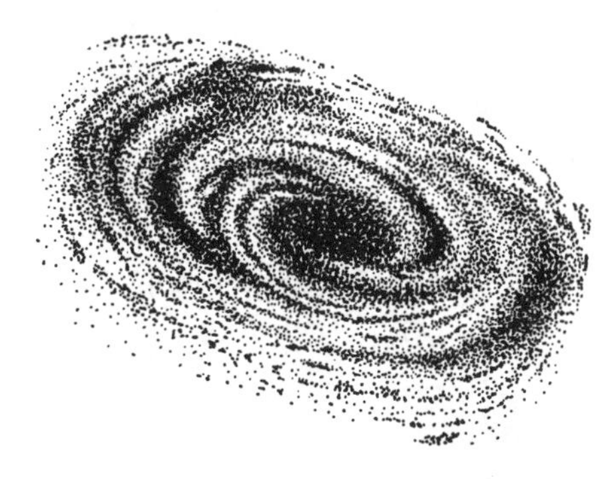

   - Ⓕ spiral
   - Ⓖ elliptical
   - Ⓗ irregular
   - Ⓙ Magellanic

3. **Stars form in clouds of dust and gas called ________ .**
   - Ⓐ nebulae
   - Ⓑ red giants
   - Ⓒ supernovas
   - Ⓓ white dwarfs

4. **A star that suddenly increases in brightness and then fades again is a ________ .**
   - Ⓕ nova
   - Ⓖ nebula
   - Ⓗ protostar
   - Ⓙ red giant

5. **Which image includes the star pattern known as the Big Dipper?**

   Ⓐ 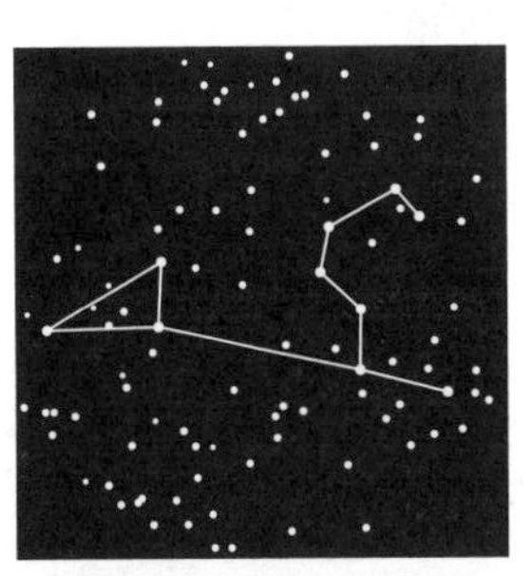

   Ⓑ 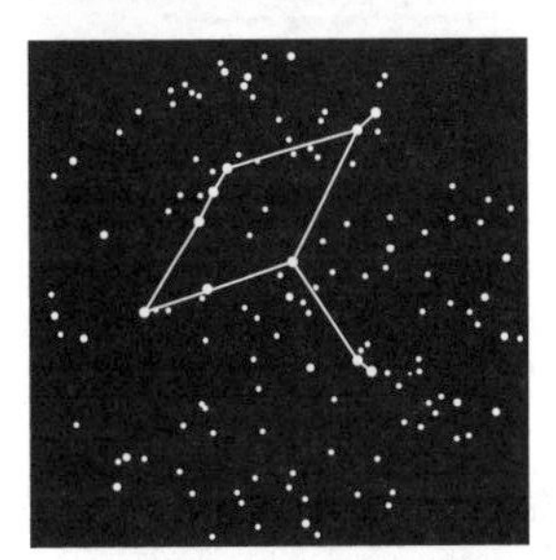

   Ⓒ 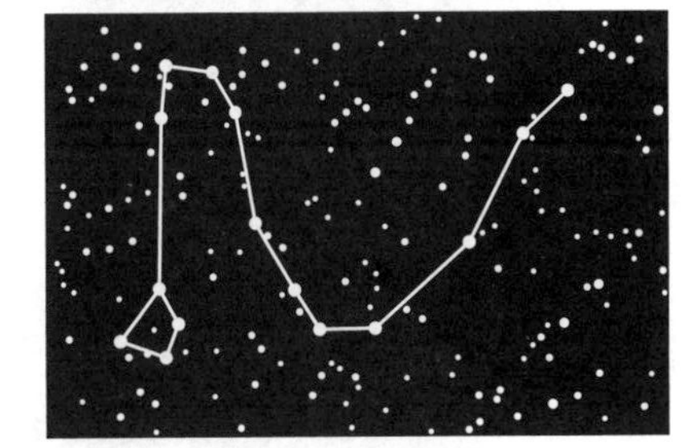

   Ⓓ 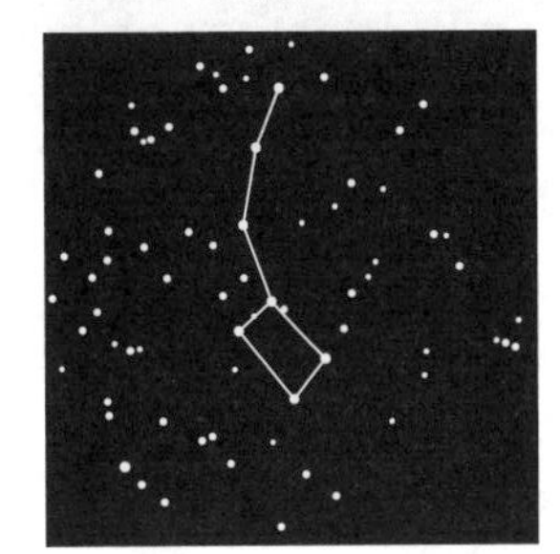

STOP

Name____ Date____________________

Grade 6

Directions: Read the questions. Choose the truest possible answer.

1. What we call a day on Earth is caused by Earth's __________ .

- (A) orbit
- (B) period
- (C) rotation
- (D) revolution

2. The amount of time it takes a planetary object to revolve around the sun is a __________ .

- (F) day
- (G) year
- (H) week
- (J) month

3. Why are the days on different planetary objects different lengths?

- (A) The planetary objects follow different orbits.
- (B) The planetary objects rotate at different speeds.
- (C) The planetary objects are different distances from the sun.
- (D) The planetary objects revolve around the sun at different speeds.

4. The movement of one object in orbit around another object is __________ .

- (F) rotation
- (G) circulation
- (H) revolution
- (J) succession

5. How long does it take the moon to go through its cycle of phases?

- (A) about a day
- (B) about a year
- (C) about an hour
- (D) about a month

6. An eclipse of the moon happens when __________ .

- (F) the moon is behind the sun
- (G) the moon is below Earth
- (H) Earth is between the moon and sun
- (J) the sun is between Earth and the moon

7. How much of the moon is seen in the first and third quarter phases?

- (A) half circle
- (B) none
- (C) one-quarter circle
- (D) three-quarters circle

STOP

Name____ Date____________________

Grade 6

Directions: Read the questions. Choose the truest possible answer.

1. What is gravity?

Ⓐ the pull that keeps the sun rotating in place

Ⓑ the power of the planets to wobble on their axes

Ⓒ the force that moves planets in the solar system

Ⓓ the attraction one object in space has on another object

2. An object will stay at rest or continue moving in a straight line because of ________ .

Ⓕ gravity

Ⓖ inertia

Ⓗ axial tilt

Ⓙ precession

3. Tides in Earth's oceans are caused by the gravity of another object in space. Which object's gravity has the greatest effect on Earth's tides?

Ⓐ Mars

Ⓑ Saturn

Ⓒ the sun

Ⓓ the moon

4. How is the gravitational pull between two objects that are close to each other different from the gravitational pull between two objects that are farther apart?

Ⓕ It is faster between the closer objects.

Ⓖ It is slower between the closer objects.

Ⓗ It is weaker between the closer objects.

Ⓙ It is stronger between the closer objects.

5. Two forces work together to keep the planets in orbit around the sun. Describe what they are and how they work together so the planets do not crash into the sun or fly off into space.

____

____

____

____

____

Name______________________________ Date______________

Grade 6 Posttest

Directions: Read the questions. Choose the truest possible answer.

1. **A prediction about an experiment is a _________ .**
   - Ⓐ variable
   - Ⓑ hypothesis
   - Ⓒ control
   - Ⓓ conclusion

2. **Which step of the scientific method comes after forming a hypothesis?**
   - Ⓕ asking a question
   - Ⓖ drawing a conclusion
   - Ⓗ planning an experiment
   - Ⓙ explaining your results

3. **Which is the best example of recording information in an experiment?**
   - Ⓐ The ball rolled quickly down the hill.
   - Ⓑ The ball stopped rolling soon after being pushed.
   - Ⓒ The ball is about 5 times as big as my hand.
   - Ⓓ The ball weighs 5 grams.

4. **Which of the following is the *least* safe behavior during an experiment?**
   - Ⓕ wearing sneakers in the lab
   - Ⓖ putting your sweater and backpack on your lab table
   - Ⓗ wearing gloves if you are touching a beaker of hot water
   - Ⓙ asking your teacher about every procedure you do not understand

5. **Hereditary information is carried in the _________ .**
   - Ⓐ genes
   - Ⓑ proteins
   - Ⓒ mitochondria
   - Ⓓ cell membranes

6. **Which two organisms are most closely related?**
   - Ⓕ those in the same class
   - Ⓖ those in the same family
   - Ⓗ those in the same phylum
   - Ⓙ those in the same order

7. **Which set of conditions will lead to seed germination?**
   - Ⓐ sufficient oxygen, hydrogen, and water
   - Ⓑ sufficient oxygen, water, and sunlight
   - Ⓒ sufficient hydrogen, water, and warmth
   - Ⓓ sufficient oxygen, water, and warmth

Name____________________ Date__________

Grade 6 Posttest

Directions: Study the chart below. Use your knowledge of science to help you fill in the blanks.

Tropism	Stimulus	Response
Positive phototropism	light	Stems bend __________ light.
Positive gravitropism	gravity	__________ grow down into soil.
Negative gravitropism	__________	Stems and shoots grow __________
__________ thigmotropism	touch	Stems bend around objects such as fence posts.

Directions: Read the questions. Choose the truest possible answer.

13. Energy enters an ecosystem through __________ .

- (F) consumers
- (G) producers
- (H) decomposers
- (J) herbivores

14. Most conifer leaves are thin and pointed and have a thick waxy covering that keeps the plant from losing water. This is an example of a(n) __________ .

- (A) angiosperm
- (B) adaptation
- (C) extinction
- (D) transpiration

15. To see a very small living thing, a scientist may use a(n) __________ .

- (F) light microscope
- (G) electron microscope
- (H) telescope
- (J) global positioning system

16. The transportation of glucose molecules to body cells is done by the __________ system.

- (A) respiratory
- (B) excretory
- (C) circulatory
- (D) muscular

GO ON

Name________________________________ Date______________

Grade 6 Posttest

Directions: Study the graph below. Use the graph to help you answer questions 17 and 18.

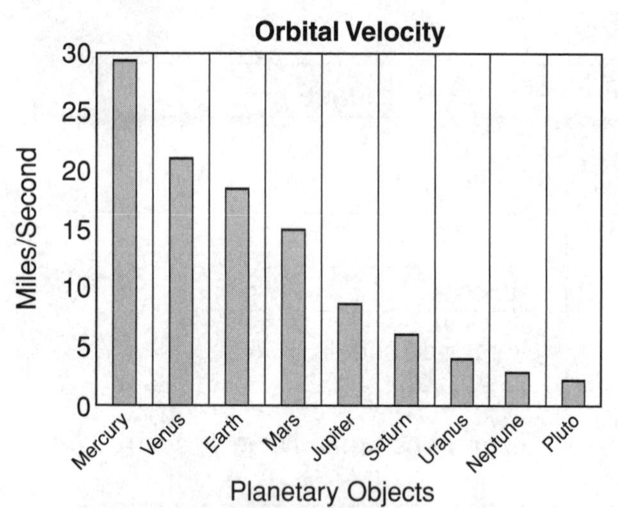

17. How fast does Earth orbit around the sun?

- (F) 29 miles per second
- (G) 21 miles per second
- (H) 18 miles per second
- (J) 15 miles per second

18. Describe the relationship between the orbital velocity of planetary objects, their distance from the sun, and the lengths of their orbits.

____

____

____

____

____

____

Directions: Explain how the sun affects life on Earth.

19.

____

____

____

____

____

____

____

____

____

____

____

____

____

____

____

____

____

____

____

____

____

____

Name______________________________ Date______________

Grade 6 Posttest

Directions: Read the questions. Choose the truest possible answer.

20. A substance that has a pH of __________ is a base.

- Ⓐ 2
- Ⓑ 5
- Ⓒ 7
- Ⓓ 10

21. In the periodic table, elements are arranged by __________ .

- Ⓕ atomic number
- Ⓖ the number of electrons
- Ⓗ atomic mass
- Ⓙ the number of neutrons

22. When a ball rolls down a hill, __________ .

- Ⓐ kinetic energy changes to potential energy
- Ⓑ potential energy changes to kinetic energy
- Ⓒ chemical energy changes to electrical energy
- Ⓓ electrical energy changes to chemical energy

23. When instant coffee is mixed with hot water, the coffee crystals are the __________ .

- Ⓕ solution
- Ⓖ solute
- Ⓗ solvent
- Ⓙ suspension

24. This pencil looks like it is bent, but it is not. What causes this to happen?

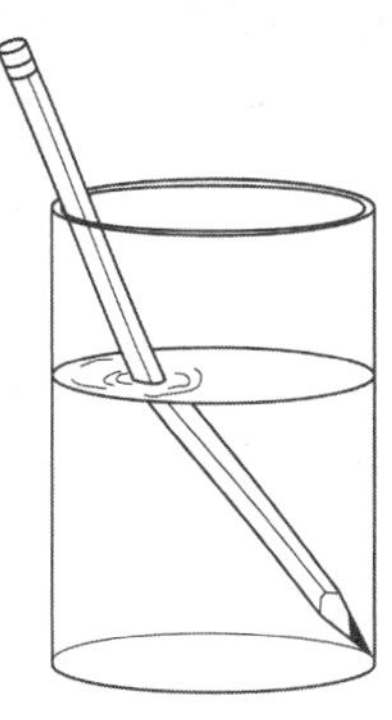

- Ⓐ refraction
- Ⓑ reflection
- Ⓒ transmission
- Ⓓ transpiration

25. What is the term for objects that light cannot travel through?

- Ⓕ opaque
- Ⓖ radiant
- Ⓗ translucent
- Ⓙ transparent

26. Which of the following types of radiation can pass through objects most easily?

- Ⓐ microwaves
- Ⓑ radio waves
- Ⓒ gamma rays
- Ⓓ x-rays

27. Which property of an object makes it tend to resist a change in motion?

- Ⓕ inertia
- Ⓖ force
- Ⓗ velocity
- Ⓙ acceleration

GO ON

Name________________________________ Date________________

Grade 6 Posttest

Directions: Read each question. Write your answers on the lines provided.

28. Elijah gives his textbook a quick shove across his desk. The book moves a short distance across the desk, but quickly slows down and stops. Explain why the book does not keep moving across the desk. Then describe how Elijah could make the textbook move farther across the desk without changing the force he exerts on it.

____

____

____

____

____

29. Suppose you want to lift a box onto a table. Compare the amount of work done if you lift it directly, push it up a ramp, or lift it with a pulley system. Explain.

____

____

____

____

____

____

____

____

Directions: Read the questions. Choose the truest possible answer.

30. What is the main job of mitochondria?

- Ⓐ to produce energy
- Ⓑ to get rid of wastes
- Ⓒ to store genetic information
- Ⓓ to package and transport materials

31. In which of these circuits does each bulb get only a fraction of the total energy?

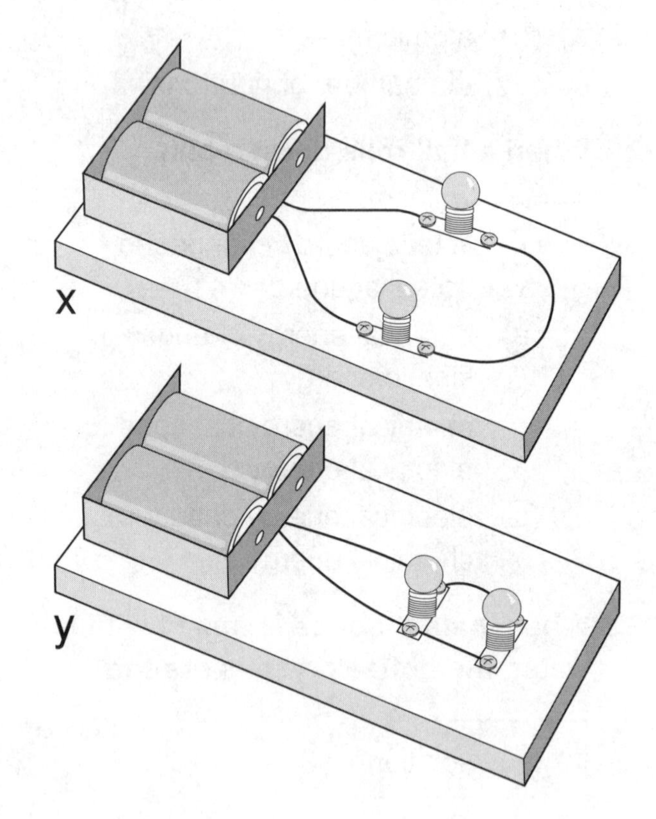

- Ⓕ X
- Ⓖ Y
- Ⓗ both
- Ⓙ neither

0-7696-8066-6—*Science Test Practice*

Name________________________________ Date______________

Grade 6 Posttest

Directions: Read the text below. Use information from the text to help you answer questions 32-35.

Akbar has a cup of hot chocolate every night before bed. Over the course of a month, he notices that his hot chocolate sometimes gets cold much faster than other times. Akbar observes that his house is usually the same temperature every night. He also notices that he sometimes uses different types of cups to drink his chocolate. He uses polystyrene, paper, metal, and ceramic cups. Akbar wonders if the type of material his cup is made of might change how fast his hot chocolate cools.

32. Akbar now wants to test the hypothesis by performing an experiment. What will be the dependent variable in Akbar's experiment?

- (A) the type of cup used
- (B) the temperature of the hot chocolate
- (C) the temperature of the house
- (D) the time Akbar goes to bed

33. Write a hypothesis that Akbar might propose.

____

____

34. Help Akbar take notes by writing a description of an experiment he might conduct. Be sure to include everything Akbar should consider in order for his experiment to be valid.

____

____

____

____

____

____

35. Now suggest a way for Akbar to record and present his results.

____

____

STOP

Page 9
1. B
2. J
3. D
4. H
5. A
6. H
7. D

Page 10
8. G
9. D
10. F
11. C
12. H
13. C

Page 11
14. T
15. F
16. T
17. F
18. F
19. T
20. T
21. T
22. T
23. F
24. F
25. F
26. F
27. T
28. F
29. T
30. F
31. F

Page 12

32. G
33. F
34. E
35. K
36. M
37. B
38. A
39. I
40. J
41. O
42. L
43. N
44. H
45. D
46. C

Page 13

47. G
48. A
49. G
50. C
51. H

Page 14
52. Natalie's mom means that plants and animals died millions of years ago, and over that time, became fossil fuels like oil, which are made into gasoline.
53. Gasoline is the energy source cars need to run, just as the lunch in Natalie's lunchbox gives her the energy to be alive and healthy.
54. Plants use sunlight to make their energy in a process called photosynthesis.
55. As water flows through the dam, it spins a generator, which produces electricity.
56. No, trees and rivers are renewable. That means they can be used again or replaced, if they are not used too quickly.

Page 15
1. The lab area is messy and unorganized. This may result in spills or pose a fire hazard.
2. An apron, gloves, and goggles should be worn.
3. a. long hair, which may pose a fire hazard
3. b. necklace, which may get caught on a piece of equipment
3. c. sandals, which leave the feet open to injury

Page 16
4, 5, 3, 2, 6, 7, 1

Page 17
1. Possible answer: She can go to a store and look at the pillows, or she could conduct research on the Internet.
2. Possible answer: The feather pillow, because it is light and will not hold as much heat.

3a. x
3b. x
3c.
3d.
4. Cotton

Page 18
1. The chart should be filled in as follows: Length: meter; Mass: kilogram; Volume: liter; Temperature: degrees Celsius; Rate of Travel: kilometer/hour
2. L, mL
3. mm
4. km
5. g
6. m
7. g, kg
8. cm

Page 19
1. C
2. H
3. C
4. F
5. C
6. H

Page 20
1. eyepiece
2. coarse-adjustment knob
3. fine-adjustment knob
4. arm
5. high-power lens
6. low-power lens
7. stage
8. light source
9. base

Page 21
1. Order of the birdseed types is unimportant. Necessary features are: relevant title, y-axis label indicating the number of bird visits, appropriate scale for y-axis, x-axis label indicating type of bird seed, and the x-axis includes all four types of seed. The four types of birdseed should be listed on the x-axis. The number of bird visits should be plotted on the y-axis. The bars should have the following values: Happy Bird Seeds: 25 visits; Yummy Seed: 20 visits; Bird's Feast Birdseed: 5 visits; Farmer Joe's Birdseed: 50 visits.

Page 22
1. B
2. J
3. A
4. G
5. B

Page 23
1. Yes, he is correct. There must be an upward force to balance the downward force of gravity, or the water would fall to the ground.
2. The force caused by his hand makes the ball move upward. The force of gravity and air resistance slows the ball as it travels upward. Gravity pulls it back down.
3. a. Steve was not able to move the desk because the force of the desk against him was stronger than the force he exerted on the desk.
   b. Steve and his brother could move the desk because their net force was greater than the force exerted by the desk.

Page 24
1. Group A
2. Group B
3. A
4. F
5. Group C
6. D

Page 25
1. Order of A and B does not matter. Also, A and B can be listed in the first column and the weeks can be listed across the top row.
   Possible answer:
   Students should create a table with four rows and three columns. The table should be filled in as follows: Row 1 Column 1: Blank; Row 1 Column 2: Fertilizer A; Row 1 Column 3: Fertilizer B; Row 2 Column 1: Week 1; Row 2 Column 2: 1 cm; Row 2 Column 3: 0.5 cm; Row 3 Column 1: Week 2; Row 3 Column 2: 3 cm; Row 3 Column 3: 1 cm; Row 4 Column 1: Week 3; Row 4 Column 2: 5 cm; Row 4 Column 3: 2 cm

Page 26
1. B
2. H
3. D
4. J

Page 27
1. D
2. J
3. C
4. G
5. C
6. G

Page 28
1. Maria could conclude that her

hypothesis is partially correct. Her pulse rate did increase after one minute of exercise, but by only about 25%, not by 50%.
2. She could repeat the experiment a few times to make sure her measurements were accurate. She should ensure her pulse rate is beating at a normal rate before beginning each trial.
3. Possible answer: Maria's increase in pulse rate may depend on the type of strenuous exercise. It may change according to her position, her environment, or her mood.
4. A bar graph of the average pulse rate at each age would clearly show the results. Each age should have two bars-one for resting pulse and one for pulse after exercising.

Page 29
1. The larger the particles of soil, the faster the water will pass through.
2. the type of soil
3. If the amounts of soil were different in the different cups, this would be an additional variable. It would not be possible to compare the rate of water movement in the different cups.

Page 30
1. Answers will vary, but students should identify their position on the matter and explain why that position was chosen.

Page 31
1. Students should give a reasonable response such as: I would design a car that could use electricity from wind energy for power. At home, you would plug in the car to an electrical outlet that stores energy created from a windmill. My source is the best because it does not produce much pollution and it is affordable for the average person.

Page 32
1. corn syrup
2. water
3. the mass of each substance
4. 9.0 g/cm^3
5. 2.7 g/cm^3
6. the wooden cube
7. lead

Page 33
1. lead, sodium chloride
2. bromine, nitric acid, octane, water
3. ammonia, oxygen
4. They move faster and faster and get farther and farther apart.
5. -57 °C
6. It will boil.

Page 34
1. The mixture could be put through a coffee filter. The sand would remain on the filter and the water would go through.
2. The magnet could be used to pick up the iron filings. Then the filings could be put in a separate place.
3. This is a suspension. A suspension occurs when the particles of a substance are dispersed throughout a liquid but not dissolved in it.
4. The mixture could be allowed to sit until all the water evaporated, leaving behind the salt; OR The mixture could be heated to boil off the water.

Page 35
1. B
2. G
3. A
4. H
5. D
6. F
7. C

Page 36
1. The terms and phrases should be distributed in the chart as follows: Metals: Luster, Good conductors, Lose electrons easily; Metalloids: Moderate conductors; Nonmetals: Poor conductors, Tend to gain electrons
2. D
3. F

Page 37
1. D
2. G
3. C
4. J
5. A
6. G

Page 38
1. Object A is moving at a constant speed. Object B is moving the same distance, but the speed is changing over time.
2. The velocity is constantly changing because the car's direction of movement is constantly changing.
3. Because object A is moving at a constant speed, it can be assumed that the object will continue to do so. After a period of six seconds, I expect object A to have traveled 36 meters. During the first four seconds, object A traveled six meters per second. I used this information to figure out the distance object A traveled in six seconds.
4. 12 km/hr
5. 20 km/hr
6. about 7 m/s

Page 39
1. Both families traveled the distance to the ocean in 4 hours, so their average speed was the same.
2. The fastest speed was 100 km/hr traveled by Darrell's family during the fourth hour of the trip.
3. 75 km/hr
4. The family's return trip had a higher average speed than the trip to the beach. The trip home probably took less time than the trip to the beach.

Page 40
1. Arrow A represents the force of the wall pushing against the car. Arrow B represents the force of the car pushing against the wall.
2. friction
3. arrow B

Page 41
1. waves
2. transverse wave
3. frequency
4. Mechanical
5. electromagnetic waves
6. radiation
7. crest
8. trough
9. compression
10. rarefaction
11. amplitude
12. wavelength

Page 42
1. D
2. F
3. C
4. H
5. B
6. F
7. D
8. G

Page 43
1. D
2. F
3. C
4. J
5. B
6. H
7. A

Page 44
1. D
2. F
3. A
4. J
5. C
6. F

Page 45
1. Equipment to collect solar energy can be expensive. This will increase the short-term cost to the business. However, the solar energy itself may ultimately be cheaper than paying for other sources of energy every month. Also, solar energy is a clean source of energy, so it will eliminate pollution. This will reduce the risk of government fees and restrictions. The lack of pollution will also help the environment over time.
2. Solar energy is always available and easy to capture for satellites and telescopes. If they were powered by a fossil fuel, they would need to be refueled somehow.

Page 46
1. ribosomes
2. mitochondrion
3. nucleus
4. nucleolus
5. nuclear membrane
6. cytoplasm
7. vacuole
8. cell membrane
9. cell wall
10. cell membrane
11. vacuole
12. nucleus
13. nucleolus
14. nuclear membrane
15. chloroplast
16. mitochondrion
17. cytoplasm

18. ribosomes

Page 47
1. D
2. F
3. C
4. F
5. A
6. H
7. D

Page 48
1. A
2. J
3. B
4. G
5. C

Page 49
1. C
2. J
3. A
4. F
5. Skin tissue provides a barrier for the body's internal organs.
6. Cells are specialized to do different jobs. Cells in heart tissue help the heart pump blood. Cells in bone tissue give your body structure.
7. Muscle tissue contracts, then joints and bones attached to muscle change position. This results in movement.

Page 50
1. C
2. G
3. B
4. H
5. A
6. The lungs take in oxygen and breathe out carbon dioxide. The oxygen moves from the lungs to the rest of the body through the blood.
7. Possible answer: The brain controls movements. The brain produces electrical signals, which allows parts of the body to communicate with each other. It also stores information as memories.

Page 51
1. C
2. H
3. D
4. G
5. D
6. J
7. Possible answers: Alice's second sickness could not be cured by antibiotics; the sickness the second time was not caused by a bacteria; the doctor felt her illness was not bad enough to need antibiotics.

Page 52
1. asexual reproduction
2. pistil
3. chlorophyll
4. sperm
5. pollinate
6. stems
7. gymnosperms
8. chloroplasts
9. stamen
10. ovules
11. sugar
12. fruit
13. pollen

Page 53
1. B
2. F
3. A
4. H
5. D
6. G
7. B

Page 54
1. C
2. F
3. Bones give the body shape and structure. Muscles attached to the bones contract and move the different bones in your body. Your muscles work together to move certain bones so you can move.
4. The respiratory system takes in air containing oxygen through the nose. The air travels to the lungs through the trachea. The lungs take oxygen out of the air. The heart pumps blood to the lungs where it picks up oxygen. The blood is pumped out of the heart through the aorta to the cells.

Page 55
1. C
2. F
3. D
4. F
5. D
6. G
7. B

Page 56
1. B
2. F
3. D
4. The Punnett square should be labeled as follows: bottom left: outside-b, inside-Bb; top left: outside left-B, outside top B, inside-BB; top right: outside-BB, inside BB; bottom right: inside Bb.

Page 57
1. An inherited trait is a trait that is passed down through your genes like your hair color or eye color. You cannot change an inherited trait. A learned behavior is one you have learned from your environment. It can be changed.
2. Possible answer: My eyes are blue like my mother's and father's. This is a trait that was passed on to me through my genes. Nothing in my environment made my eyes blue. I was born this way.
3. Picking up the food with a fork to put it in my mouth is a learned behavior. I learned to use a fork by watching people around me use utensils and learning from them. Chewing and swallowing my food is an instinctual behavior. I did not have to be taught to chew and swallow food. People automatically know they need to eat.
4. Possible learned behavior: A learned behavior that I do is folding my clothes before I put them in a drawer. I learned this from my father. He always makes sure everything gets folded before it is put away.

Page 58
1. environment
2. biotic
3. abiotic
4. habitat
5. population
6. community
7. decomposers
8. ecosystem
9. sunlight
10. producers
11. consumers
12. niche

Page 59
1. consumer
2. producer
3. decomposer
4. consumer
5. consumer
6. producer
7. decomposer
8. consumer

Page 60
1. The arrows represent the flow of energy in the ecosystem.
2. The tree is the producer. It is eaten by the grasshopper, the birds, the mouse, and the fox.
3. Possible answer: The fox and the owl are competing for mice.

Page 61
1. B
2. J
3. D
4. F

Page 62
1. B
2. G
3. D
4. J
5. C
6. G
7. C

Page 63
1. Answers will vary, but students should indicate that having a strong immune system is very important because there are many threats to the body in addition to cuts and bruises. Pollution has created many small threats that the body has to fight off without people ever knowing about it. This includes dirtier air and water, which the immune system must work to protect the body from. It also includes litter in populated areas, which makes germs a growing problem. In addition to these environmental factors, new sicknesses and diseases are always in the news, reminding people of new medical threats all over the world. Even conditions as ordinary as allergies and sunburn can be very dangerous. The body has to work constantly to fight off old and new invaders.

Page 64
1. B

2. G
3. C
4. G
5. D
6. H
7. Answers will vary, but students should mention that brushing and flossing prevents the build up of plaque, and promotes healthy gums.

Page 65
1. B
2. J
3. B
4. J
5. A
6. H
7. grains, vegetables, fruits, dairy, meats, and fats and oils

Page 66
1. D
2. G
3. A; An instinct, such as following a parent, is an inborn pattern of behavior. The other diagrams represent actions that are learned.

Page 67
1. Answers will vary, but should mention how adaptation is based on the needs of animals within a habitat. Students should discuss ways that adaptations help animals survive. Students may cite examples such as blending into surroundings in order to escape from predators, ways to keep warm in cold climates, and ways of hunting or obtaining food. Answers should discuss at least one example from the passage, and incorporate relevant outside knowledge.

Page 68
1. They need to find a way to get or conserve water, and survive extreme climate.
2. No, it could not. It would lose too much water though the openings in its leaves, and it would dry out.
3. The plant can complete its entire life cycle when water is available. It does not need to deal with getting or storing water during a dry spell. Also, because the plant only germinates in the spring, its offspring stand a better chance of survival.

Page 69
1. Answers will vary, but students should explain that, although extinction occurs naturally, the rate of extinction increases because of human activities. They should discuss how hunting, pollution, and destruction of natural habitats leads to extinction. They may cite a specific member of a species that is extinct or endangered, and explain why. They may also extend their response to include ways to curb the extinction rate and/or protect endangered species.

Page 70
1. It takes millions of years for the sediments that contain the preserved remains of an organism to turn into rock.
2. Possible answer: The animal froze to death during a snow storm. More and more snow fell. The snow never melted, but instead turned to ice. The animal's body remained trapped in the ice. The ice melted, revealing the animal.
3. Possible answers: information about organisms that no longer exist; how life evolves; how different species are related; how organisms are affected by their environment; changes in geography.

Page 71
1. inner core
2. outer core
3. mantle
4. asthenosphere
5. lithosphere
6. crust
7. crust
8. inner core
9. outer core
10. lithosphere

Page 72
1. B
2. J
3. B
4. F
5. A

Page 73
1. B
2. H
3. B
4. J

Page 74
1. A seed finds its way into a crack in the rocks, where it sprouts and begins to grow. As the tree grows, its roots grow down into the crack in the rock. As the roots get larger, they cause the rock to break apart.
2. Erosion will occur at points 2, 4, and 5, at the outside of each bend, where the moving water flows against the river bank and pulls sediments away with it.
3. Wind carrying tiny particles eroded most of the rock. However, some of the rock was not eroded and remained to form the arch.
4. When water freezes in a crack in a rock, the water expands. This can break the rock apart. Also, in areas where daytime temperatures are high and nighttime temperatures are low, the heating and cooling of the rock can cause sheets of rock to break off.

Page 75

a. igneous rocks; b. sediments; c. melting; d. deposition; e. metamorphic rocks; f. sedimentary rocks

Page 76
1. Drawing of any method should be labeled, and should include the significant parts of that method. For example, a drawing of strip-cropping should include at least two different types of crops, like corn and wheat that are in alternating rows on a hill.

Page 77
1. Condensation occurs at A, and evaporation occurs at D. In both cases, liquid water changes to water vapor. Evaporation is the process of liquid changing into a gas. Condensation is the process of water vapor changing into a liquid.
2. Precipitation in the form of rain, snow, sleet, hail, or freezing rain occurs at point B. This causes runoff, which returns water to lakes, streams, and oceans.
3. D
4. Answers will vary, but should explain ways that our fresh water supply is limited, like pollution, overuse, and growing demand.

Page 78
1. atmosphere
2. temperature
3. troposphere
4. stratosphere
5. ozone
6. mesosphere
7. thermosphere
8. exosphere
9. space
10. helium
11. C
12. G

Page 79
1. cumulus
2. cumulonimbus
3. cirrus
4. stratus
5. cirrocumulus
6. Cirrus clouds form high in the atmosphere where it is very cold. They are thin and wispy. They are made of ice crystals and do not usually result in precipitation. Cumulus clouds form close to Earth. They are high and puffy. They also do not result in precipitation.
7. No. Cirrus clouds are caused by warm fronts. Cold fronts cause thunderstorms. Leanna should not see cirrus clouds if there will be thunderstorms later on.

Page 80
1. B
2. F
3. A
4. G
5. A

Page 81
1. Mercury
2. Venus
3. Earth
4. Mars
5. Jupiter
6. Saturn
7. Uranus
8. Neptune
9. Pluto
10. Other objects in our solar system include moons, comets, asteroids, meteoroids, meteors, dwarf planets, etc.

Page 82
1. B
2. H

3. A
4. F
5. A

Page 83
1. B
2. F
3. A
4. F
5. D

Page 84
1. C
2. G
3. B
4. H
5. D
6. H
7. A

Page 85
1. D
2. G
3. D
4. J
5. Possible answer: Gravity and inertia work together to keep the planetary objects orbiting the sun. The planets are moving because of inertia. Inertia by itself would make the planetary objects move in a straight line. Gravity from the sun causes the planetary objects to move in a curved path. Gravity and inertia work against each other so the planetary objects do not crash into the sun or fly off into space.

Page 86
1. B
2. G
3. D
4. G
5. A
6. G
7. D

Page 87
8. toward
9. roots
10. gravity
11. up (away from soil)
12. positive
13. G
14. B
15. F
16. C

Page 88
17. H
18. The closer the planet is to the sun, the shorter its orbit and faster its orbital velocity.
19. The sun heats Earth and provides us with light. It provides the energy that green plants use to make food from carbon dioxide and water, which is the basis of most food chains on Earth and to give off oxygen, which most organisms need to live. It causes evaporation of water and precipitation to fall. The precipitation is needed for life on Earth. This cycle is what sustains the life of most organisms.

Page 89
20. D
21. F
22. B
23. G
24. A
25. F
26. C
27. F

Page 90
28. Friction between the book and the table acts against the applied force, which makes the book slow down and stop; to make the book move farther, Elijah could apply a lubricant such as oil to the book or table.
29. The amount of work required would be the same in all three cases. Work = force x distance, and although in each case the force is applied differently, the weight of the box does not change. Therefore, the amount of work in the end is the same.
30. C
31. F

Page 91
32. B
33. Answers should state either the general idea that the material the cup is made of will determine how fast the hot chocolate cools, or it can be more specific, like "the polystyrene cup will make the hot chocolate cool the fastest."
34. The experiment should involve using a thermometer to measure how fast hot chocolate will cool when contained by each of the different types of cups over a set period of time. Answer should include discussion about making the type of cup the only variable by keeping other factors (such as temperature of the room, amount of hot chocolate) the same.
35. To keep his information organized, Akbar should record his results in a table. In order to present his results, he should put his data in a line graph that clearly shows how type of cup affects temperature of a liquid over time.